BOOKS BY GARY ALLEN

Communist Revolution in the Streets
Richard Nixon: The Man Behind The Mask
Nixon's Palace Guard
*None Dare Call It Conspiracy**
*The Rockefeller File**
*Kissinger: The Secret Side of the
    Secretary of State**

(*available in paperbound from '76 Press)

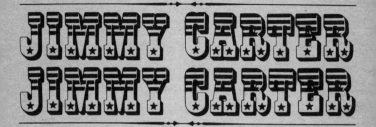

JIMMY CARTER JIMMY CARTER

by Gary Allen

'76 PRESS

Seal Beach, California

Published by

'76 Press

P.O. Box 2686

Seal Beach, Calif. 90740

Copyright © 1976 by '76 Press

First printing, August 1976

International Standard Book Number 0-89245-006-1
Library of Congress Catalog Card Number 76-27187

MANUFACTURED IN THE UNITED STATES OF AMERICA

CONTENTS

ACKNOWLEDGMENT

This is to express my thanks to all those who so ably assisted in the preparation of this book, especially Jo Ludwig, for her monumental efforts at research, and my very good friend, Wally Wood, who conceived the project, saw that it never faltered, and whose influence can be felt on virtually every page. Without them this book would not have been possible.

1 The Democrats' Love-in

The first Democratic Convention in New York City in fifty-two years was as unlike the riotous conflict in Miami four years earlier as a prayer meeting is different from a protest march. Gone were the shouted obscenities from the convention floor; the plastic bags of excrement and razor blades hurled at "the pig police;" and the frantic gyrations of the Yippies and other revolutionaries.

The Fun City convention this hot, muggy mid-July was virtually an oasis of calm and confidence. George McGovern's suicidal campaign four years ago, on behalf of "amnesty, abortion, and acid," had vanished into an Orwellian memory hole. And most of the five-thousand delegates and alternates to this year's convention preferred it that way.

The Democratic standard bearer for 1976 had been acknowledged weeks before the convention. For over a year the pollsters and pundits had predicted that this convention would be wide open — a heated battle between several declared candidates, while such noncandidates as Hubert Humphrey and Ted Kennedy licked their lips on the sidelines in anticipation of a stalemate. But a peanut farmer from rural Georgia surprised them all. James Earl Carter, Jr., known to everyone as Jimmy, had stunned the experts by walking off with all the marbles more than five weeks earlier.

Frank Church, Henry Jackson, Mo Udall, *et al* still

had their warm-up jackets on when the referees announced that Jimmy had won the game. Poor Hubert Humphrey was still in the clubhouse, trying to decide whether to don track shoes or loafers, when he heard the news. With a sob in his throat and tears in his eyes, he declared that he was simply delighted and thrilled and pleased as punch with the result. Sure, Hubert. And Richard Nixon was overjoyed with Watergate.

With the outcome of the convention obvious six weeks in advance, the Democrat's meeting in New York had all of the suspense of a Carrie Nation pamphlet on booze. Genial Jimmy, who had already dealt himself a royal flush, tried to maintain some interest in the bidding by announcing he would not reveal his selection for Vice President until he himself formally was handed the Presidential scepter. Then he had each potential nominee for the office come visit him in Plains, Georgia, or his suite in the Americana Hotel in New York, for a good ol' chat.

The delegates waited patiently through the opening session on Monday, July 12; the acceptance, with hardly a murmur of dispute, of this year's party platform on Tuesday; and the nomination, by acclamation, of Jimmy Carter on Wednesday. Finally, on Thursday morning came the only surprise of the affair. But what a surprise it turned out to be! Jimmy had reached way into the left-field bleachers of the U.S. Senate and plucked Walter Mondale to be his running mate. Mr. Peanut was teamed with Mr. Bussing for the race — and the pollsters immediately declared the Democratic candidates were twelve-point favorites over *any* team the Republicans could field in Kansas City one month later.

As a reporter covering the sessions for a national magazine, I had been mingling with the delegates and party officials for nearly a week. Their mood of euphoric optimism was unmistakable; they *knew* they had a winner. The message from on high was equally clear: Don't rock the boat, don't ask embarrassing questions, don't make any unnecessary noise . . . and we'll swamp the demoralized Republicans in November.

The rank-and-file was looking forward to an election that would revenge the horrible embarrassment of 1972, when the national ticket carried but a single state. Moreover, the party pros had already seen the results of a private Carter poll which showed that the Democrats could gain an additional thirty seats in the House of Representatives — giving them a nearly three-to-one majority over the Republicans. The very thought made the brass rub their hands in glee.

The New York show was not a convention, it was a love-in. Old battles were forgotten as delegates munched happily on Southern-fried chicken and peanut butter sandwiches, and dreamed about the swirl of crinolines at the Inaugural Ball.

As I drifted from group to group on the floor of Madison Square Garden, there was only one question that I heard repeated again and again: What will Jimmy *do* when he wins? Every special-interest group had already claimed Carter as their own. The labor unions were as delighted as the small farmers; teachers were already thinking of ways to spend the big boost in federal funds they were sure would be theirs under a Carter Administration; social workers counted on a huge increase in welfare benefits; conservationists sighed at the thought of blue skies, clear water, and silent factories. Blacks, Chicanos, women's libbers and gays, one worlders and pacifists had all been privately assured that Jim Boy was playing for their team.

But behind the confident smiles, the glad cries, and the faked enthusiasm of the carefully rehearsed spontaneous demonstrations, a trace of uneasiness could be detected. Who *is* this man with the Ultra Brite smile? Where did he come from? How did he do it? And even more important, what will a Carter victory *mean* for America?

Jimmy Carter just smiled and smiled and smiled. "Trust me," he told them . . . and they wanted to, and they did. TRB, writing in *The New Republic* two months earlier, described the same phenomenon at a Carter rally in Pennsylvania:

> With this man Jimmy Carter I don't know whether the country is having a presidential election or a religious revival. He took his windup campaign in Pennsylvania to the site of the Liberty Bell and waived adieu to a crowd of 250. "I love every one of you," he called. I think there have been few elections in our history with the overtones of this one, after Vietnam and Richard Nixon. I am confident there has never been a serious presidential candidate before like Jimmy Carter . . . .
>
> My impression is that audiences yearn to believe Jimmy Carter. They yearn to believe — and after the results in the Pennsylvania primary last week — we must conclude that substantial numbers of voters in a large industrial state are preparing to take a chance in our strange presidential lottery.

The Democratic delegates in New York said, as everyone knew they would, "I believe." And Jimmy Carter emerged from the quietest convention in memory as the odds-on favorite to win the Presidency this fall. In the process, as the *Los Angeles Times* reported, he wrote "a new chapter in American political history."

It was on December 12, 1974, that James Earl Carter, Jr. announced he was a candidate for the Presidential nomination. To say that he was an unknown would be to exaggerate his reputation. Georgia's largest newspaper, the *Atlanta Constitution*, greeted the news with an editorial that was headlined, "Jimmy Carter Running for What?" Most of the nation's press didn't even bother to give the announcement an inch of space.

But Jimmy was neither surprised nor dismayed. He and a small circle of advisers were following a brilliantly planned script. They knew *exactly* what they were doing and how far they were going; the target was the White House.

The plan was conceived in 1972, when Carter was less than halfway through a four-year term as governor of Georgia. The peanut politico from southwest Georgia had first nibbled on the heady fruits of national politics a few months earlier, at the Democratic National Convention in Miami. There were vague murmurs that Carter might be amenable to the number-two spot on the ticket, under that madcap leftist George McGovern. Carter's hints went unheeded, which was probably just as well. Any political ambitions he harbored would have been buried in the rubble of McGovern's disastrous defeat.

On July 25, 1972, an aide to Governor Carter, Peter Bourne, submitted a memo to the boss suggesting that he consider running for the Presidency in 1976. Many men with a larger national reputation would have blushed at such a premature proposal, but the British psychiatrist knew his man; Carter admitted that such an idea had already crossed his mind once or twice.

During the next five months, Carter strategists researched every Presidential election since World War II. They ordered detailed studies of voting trends and population patterns in every Congressional district; they read virtually every major book about Presidents and presidential campaigns. They had charts and graphs and surveys galore. And by November 1972, Carter's executive secretary, Hamilton Jordan (who would later emerge as campaign manager for Mr. Jimmy in Carter's blitz of the 1976 primaries), had drafted a seventy-page outline of the campaign strategy to follow during the next four years.

It is a measure of the brilliance of the original plan that only minor modifications were made from the time it was first prepared until Jimmy Carter was handed the Democratic nomination on a platter in New York City.

Despite his carefully crafted image as a plain-spoken farmer from rural Georgia — jus' folks, like y'all — for the past fourteen years Carter has been, first and foremost, a politician. A very successful and exceedingly adroit politician, we might add.

By now, almost everyone knows about Carter's background and his meteoric rise in national politics. A graduate of the U.S. Naval Academy, he served in the Navy from 1947 to 1953. He returned to Georgia upon the death of his father and set about expanding the family's farm supply business. He became chairman of the local school board and first president of the Georgia Planning Association. Then, in 1962, Jimmy Carter decided to run for public office. He campaigned for the State Senate. The first returns from that election indicated that he had lost the race, but Carter had spotted some voting irregularities in one district. When the county Democratic chairman refused to look into his charges, Carter went to the press and demanded an investigation. A subsequent inquiry showed that at least one box was stuffed with ballots signed by "voters" who were dead, in jail, or had moved out of the area. Carter was given the Democratic nomination for the seat, which was tantamount to election.

Carter served in the Georgia Senate for four years without particular distinction. Then, in 1966 he decided that he was ready for a higher calling. That year he ran for Governor as a strict segregationist — at one point boasting, "I'm a redneck" — but was soundly beaten in the Democratic primary. He vowed at the time that it was the last election he would ever lose. "I waited about one month and then began campaigning again for governor," Carter later recalled in his campaign autobiography, *Why Not The Best?* "I remembered the admonition, 'You show me a good loser and I'll show you a loser.' I did not intend to lose again."

For the past ten years — ever since that 1966 defeat at the polls — Carter has known exactly what he has wanted, where he is going, and how he is going to get there. He has proven that he is a tireless campaigner, often working eighteen hours a day, six days a week, for months on end. He does not intend to come in second-best in *any* contest.

In the 1970 race for Governor, Carter estimates that he and his wife shook the hands of some 600,000 persons — about half the registered voters in Georgia. During the long primary trail of 1976, Jimmy and his family easily exceeded that figure as they travelled the country day and night for almost eighteen months. More than any other candidate, Carter overwhelmed the voters with personal appearances, sophisticated TV ads, and slick mailing pieces. The only candidate to enter almost every primary (Carter ran in 30 of the 31 Democratic primaries, avoiding only West Virginia), the down-home boy with the kilowatt bicuspids and soft Georgia drawl received more media publicity than all other Democratic candidates combined. (Even before the Democratic convention, he had been on the cover of *Newsweek* twice and *Time* three times.)

There is probably not a single person in America who can read or write who has not heard about Jimmy Carter's phenomenal rise to political stardom. He has shaken the hands of more voters in the past six months than any other candidate for any office in the country. His campaign has been covered with the moment-by-moment, mile-by-mile attention accorded man's first walk on the moon. In a word, Jimmy Carter has gotten exposure. Lots of it.

And yet, with more media publicity than Elizabeth Taylor's marriages, the man himself remains an enigma. A survey by the Roper Organization for *Associated Press* this June revealed that only one Carter supporter in five could correctly identify the Governor's position on the important issues; nearly two-thirds of those questioned indicated that their support was based on "personal qualities," not on issues anyway.

Syndicated columnist Joseph C. Harsch tried to analyze Jimmy Carter's amazing ability to appeal to everyone while offending no one:

> *Jimmy Carter has been masterful in the art of avoiding antagonizing any large segment of voters. He has done well both in black and in white ethnic wards. Blue-collar workers who followed Wallace have turned to Carter, but so too have blacks. No one group of people feels that he is against them and their kind. He isn't against anyone. He has managed to keep his balance between whites and blacks, between taxpayers and welfare receivers, between those who would make high employment the first task of government and those who fear inflation more than unemployment.*

The strategy, of course, is not new. Nearly a century ago Mark Twain wrote that anyone could run for

President, and probably win, on a short speech he had written for any candidate who would use it: "I am in favor of everything anybody is in favor of. What you should do is satisfy the whole nation, not half of it, for then you would only be half of a President. There could not be a broader platform than mine. I am in favor of anything and everything — of temperance and intemperance, morality and qualified immorality, gold standard and free silver."

Jimmy Carter has simply applied these ageless principles to the political campaigns of the 1970s. To his credit, he has done it better than anyone else.

Margaret Costanza, Vice Mayor of Rochester, New York and Carter's campaign leader in the state, gloats: "He's a conservative to conservatives, a moderate to moderates, a liberal to liberals. Jimmy Carter has believability!" Yes, if a successful effort to be all things to all people makes you believable, the man who was so richly blessed by the Tooth Fairy has got it.

It is possible that Carter can continue to talk his way over, under, around, and through the thorniest of issues until this November. While Abe Lincoln said that you can't fool all of the people all of the time, he did admit you can fool all of the people some of the time, and some of the people all of the time. If Carter can remain aloof but loving, vague but compassionate, uncontroversial but sincere until the elections, he is almost certain to be the next President of these United States.

There is just one problem with such a strategy. Carter has already declared himself on several important issues. The Democratic platform commits him to many more. His record as governor of Georgia is available for public scrutiny. And as the campaign progresses, he undoubtedly will be forced to address himself to more and more policies.

During the second week of July, I interviewed scores of delegates at the Democratic Convention. I listened to the nominating speeches, the seconding speeches, the reports and the declarations, until I was numb. And I came away from the Democrats' love-in very disturbed. Disturbed because I knew there was so much more to the Carter record than has been revealed thus far. Disturbed that so many people would wax so enthusiastic about a candidate they admit they know so little about. And disturbed because of the astounding success of a tousle-haired politician who says simply, "Trust me. I'll never lie to you."

"Trust me. I'll never lie to you." Jimmy Carter's campaign rhetoric sounds good. But is it too good to be true?

2 The Making Of A Winner

In 1966 Jimmy Carter finished a poor third in his campaign for Governor of Georgia. He ran as a conservative who was pro-segregation and anti-big government. Despite the rhetoric, apparently the voters found him too liberal; there were rumors that Kennedy money was behind his candidacy, and he was defeated by the former restauranteur and ardent Americanist, Lester Maddox.

Within a month, Carter had launched his campaign for the governor's office in 1970. By law in Georgia, an incumbent governor may not succeed himself. Carter knew that Maddox could be an invaluable ally four years later, so Jimmy made certain he kept his fences carefully mended and gleamingly white-washed.

Carter's chief opponent in the 1970 Democratic primary was former Governor Carl Sanders, a slick, big-city lawyer who ran as an avowed liberal. Carter ran as a hard-nosed conservative. "I was never a liberal; I am and have always been a conservative," he repeated over and over again. To make sure the voters got the message, he promised that one of his first acts as governor would be to invite George Wallace to address the state legislature. He told one reporter, "I'm basically a redneck." And he happily accepted the endorsement of Roy Harris, Wallace's campaign manager in the state and head of the Citizens' Council.

It was during this campaign that the Carter team first

perfected the sophisticated use of the media, especially television commercials, that has become a feature of the Carter race for the Presidency. Jimmy was shown dressed in jeans and boots, shoveling peanuts in the hot Georgia sun, while he blasted his opponent as "Cuff Links Carl." One Carter TV commercial showed a man wearing huge cuff links stepping out of a private jet and accepting a bucketful of cash. Carter — who worked in an air-conditioned office, not the fields, and by this time may have been worth more money than Sanders — repeatedly told audiences that *the* issue of the campaign was Sanders' integrity and "how he got rich so fast."

Another Carter TV commercial featured a Sanders' campaign button. As a cloth was rubbed over it, Sanders' face disappeared and the smiling visage of Hubert Humphrey took its place; a sepulchral voice solemnly warned Georgians that Sanders was really a Humphrey Democrat. Horrors!

Carter accused Sanders of maintaining a secret list of fat-cat contributors to whom he had promised big favors once he was elected. Carter never substantiated the charge; and, when he was pressed to release a list of his own contributors, he flatly refused. (The list is still unavailable today.)

Jimmy accused Sanders of selling out to "the northern unions," and warned that Sanders would repeal the state's right-to-work law if he were elected. After he won the election, it proved to be Carter, not Sanders, who favored making union membership compulsory.

But these underhanded tactics were just "politics as usual," compared to some of the dirty tricks the Carter campaign had up its sleeves. One group prepared an anonymous leaflet which showed Sanders, who had been an owner of the Atlanta Hawks basketball team, being doused with champagne by two of the team's black players during a victory celebration. The leaflet showing this "champagne shampoo" being given by blacks to a white candidate for governor was mailed to rural ministers and white barbershops across the state.

Carter denied having anything to do with the scurrilous mailing, but an Atlanta public-relations man who worked for Gerald Rafshoon, Carter's media director, later admitted: "We distributed that leaflet. It was prepared by Bill Pope, who was then Carter's press secretary. It was part of an operation we called 'the stink tank.'" (Pope said after the campaign that the Carter strategy was simply to "out-redneck the rednecks.")

The man who campaigned as a friend of blacks in 1976 made it clear in 1970 that he couldn't care less if he received their votes. He pasted himself like a second skin to Lester Maddox, an enormously popular vote-getter who was running for Lieutenant Governor.* Carter repeated over and over again that he was "proud to have Lester Maddox as my running mate" and that Maddox represented "the essence of the Democratic party."

In 1976, Maddox called Carter, "one of the most intellectually dishonest men I have ever known." With his aplomb intact, Jimmy replied, "Being called a liar by Lester Maddox is like being called ugly by a frog." It was another calculated Carter comeback. No one bothered to report that even Lester's most ardent critics, who loath his hard-headed conservatism, admit that Maddox never told a lie or even exaggerated the truth while in office. On the contrary, he was always painfully honest about his views — unlike his successor.

Five days before the 1970 election, Carter made a widely publicized visit to a private, all-white academy. The school had been established after the forced inte-

---

* Maddox won his race by taking 73 percent of the votes cast; Carter was elected by the much smaller majority of 60 percent.

gration of the public schools, and there was no doubt what Jimmy meant when he said he was there "to reassure Georgians of my support for private education."

There was a third candidate in the race for governor that year: a black lawyer named C. B. King. King's prospects of being elected were about as good as those of a tomato farm in the Sahara. Since his campaign was woefully under-financed, expensive TV and radio ads were out of the question. Realizing that Carter would receive almost no black support, and that a vote for King was therefore a vote taken away from Sanders, the Carter people simply moved in and ran King's media campaign. Ray Abernathy, who worked on the Carter advertising campaign, later said:

> *Carter's campaign financed King's media advertising. I personally prepared all of King's radio ads while I was on Rafshoon's payroll and supervised the production. And I helped channel money to the company Rafshoon used to pay for them.*

When asked about Abernathy's charges, King said, "I never knew specifically of that, but it could have happened . . . . I found out later on that I was naive, and a lot of crass and evil people helped me for the wrong reasons."

It was an amazing performance for a man who later said that one of his biggest problems as a politician is that "I find it impossible to compromise on principle." Ah, well. The "principle" in 1970 was to get Carter elected, and he didn't have to compromise on that after all. He won handily. With his victory clinched, Carter promptly proved he could change faces faster than Dr. Jekyll turning into Mr. Hyde.

During the campaign for Governor, Carter had privately told a black leader in Atlanta, "You won't like my campaign, but you'll be proud of my record as governor." He had already proven the truth of the first part of that statement; during his inaugural address he confirmed the second.

Jimmy Carter surprised most of his audience at his inaugural address when he declared, "I say to you quite frankly that the time for racial discrimination is past." It was not the words themselves that were a shock; it was the man who delivered them. Was this the self-proclaimed "redneck" who had campaigned as an ardent segregationist?

Carter's inaugural address was just the beginning of one of the most incredible switches since Christine Jorgenson's sex operation. Later, he stunned friends and foes alike by proclaiming Martin Luther King, Jr. Day in Georgia, and announcing that he would hang a portrait of King in the capitol building. While leftist rewriters of history have convinced many Americans that King embodies all the saintly virtues, a lot of Georgians knew the truth: King was a moral degenerate and lying agitator who had worked closely with Communists to spark some of the bloodiest riots in our history.

No matter what the truth was yesterday. Today is what counts to Jimmy Carter — and what it will bring tomorrow. While the Ku Klux Klan picketed outside, and inside a crowd raised the black power salute and sang "We Shall Overcome," the portrait went up.

Carter's switch to being an ardent integrationist and civil rights advocate was not total; in 1972 he endorsed a gerrymandered apportionment scheme for the three districts in Atlanta that virtually assured no black candidate could win any of the seats. And he has supported changes in the application of the Voting Rights Act of 1965 that civil rights leaders said would dilute its effects.

Nevertheless, his change of heart — or at least of

politics — was substantial enough so that by 1976, one of his most enthusiastic supporters was Andrew Young, Jr., a former assistant to Martin Luther King, Jr. in the riot-provoking days of King's Southern Christian Leadership Conference. Young, now a Congressman from Atlanta, stumped the country for Carter during this year's primaries. (Although it is interesting that Young did *not* support Carter during either of his campaigns for governor of Georgia.)

But the most ardent supporter of Jimmy's new image was his mother, a peripatetic lady known far and wide as Miss (now Miz) Lillian. The salty septugenarian describes herself as "the most liberal woman in Georgia." And she adds: "I have always tried to be tolerant — even of people from Alabama."

Back in 1966, Miss Lillian — then a young 68 — decided to go somewhere "I could be of service to people who had nothing." She joined the Peace Corps and specifically asked to be sent to "a dark country with a warm climate." Why a "dark" country? "Because of my feeling that the South had been so terrible to minorities." After nine months of training she was sent to India, where she proved to be as stormy an influence as she had been in Plains. (Reflecting once on her life in rural Georgia, she said: "Everyone knows I am an integrationist. I get tired of explaining. My feelings are so different from others around here. I don't have an intimate friend in this town . . . .")

After two arduous years in India, Miss Lillian returned to Georgia, weary and debilitated, but proud of the work she had done. Gloating about her success in circumventing India's officialdom, she said: "I learned how to steal and lie in India. I had to. It was my Christian duty."

Miss Lillian is an unusual Southern belle, to say the least. The July 1976 issue of *McCall's* reports one campaign incident, when a reporter loaned her a book his wife had packed for him. Learning later that the contents were "pretty lurid," he hastened to apologize. "Don't be silly," the 77-year-old matriarch replied. "I *luuuuuu-ved* it."

If Miss Lillian was the first to applaud the "new" Jimmy Carter, other — and far more significant — praise was soon to follow. The lead story in *Time* magazine of May 31, 1971 was titled "Dixie Whistles a Different Tune." And there on the cover was a full-color portrait of Georgia Governor Jimmy Carter.

The *Time* painting was vaguely reminiscent of Jack Kennedy. No wonder. We have been told that the artists commissioned to paint the cover portrait were instructed to make Carter look as much as possible like J. F. K.* At least four artists submitted as many as twenty sketches before the editors found one sufficiently Kennedyesque. Contrived? Calculated? You bet! Young Jimmy was being shown the perquisites and rewards that could be bestowed on someone who played the game according to the rules of the Establishment kingmakers. And you can be sure he got the message.

Carter was neither the most brilliant nor the most inept governor that Georgia has had. There were a number of accomplishments during his four years in office, true. But the record certainly does not justify Jim-

---

* Carter campaigners have not been adverse to promoting the resemblance of their man to the hero of PT-109, going as far as suggesting, in one brochure, that Jimmy resembles Kennedy in heart and spirit as well as in looks. There was a totally unexpected backlash to the Camelot identification, however: Rumors began to ripple across the South that Jimmy Carter was in fact the illegitimate son of Joseph Kennedy, Sr. — based on the claim that Lillian was once Kennedy's secretary. Needless to say, there is not a shred of evidence to support such a preposterous allegation. But references to Jimmy's close resemblance to Jack are no longer encouraged.

my's claim that he accomplished "a revolution in government."

The most highly publicized result of his term in office was the reorganization of the state's governmental bureaucracy. But it is significant *not* because it radically changed the nature, cost, or efficiency of state government in Georgia; it did none of these things. The issue is important today only because the Carter staff has hailed it as such a herculean accomplishment, and has promised that Jimmy will accomplish even bigger wonders when he can reorganize the bloated federal bureaucracy.

What are the facts? Jimmy claims that he fought and scrapped and "twisted some arms" to get his program of reorganization passed; as a result, Jimmy says, 278 state agencies and departments were abolished. The savings for the citizens of Georgia, we are told, amounted to more than $50 million dollars a year.

The truth is that the only boards and committees that were abolished had been dormant for years; they had not received *any* funds in the budget Carter inherited. Virtually every on-going governmental program or project in Georgia *was* continued. Carter did not inherit over 300 state agencies, as he claims. A more accurate figure is 65. Moreover, he did not abolish *any* of these bureaus; he simply created 22 *super*-agencies, and lumped all of the old departments and bureaus under them.

Carter's falsehoods about reorganization were so incredible they cost him the support of Tom Murphy, speaker of the Georgia House while Jimmy was Governor. Murphy had campaigned on Carter's behalf in both 1966 and 1970, but broke with the peanut politician over reorganization. Far from achieving "a revolution in state government," Murphy says, all Carter accomplished was "a cosmetic rearrangement of the furniture." It wasn't the only time Jimmy used lots of beauty aids to hide his political warts.

How much did the "reorganization" save the taxpayers of Georgia? The record again reveals a far different story than Carter promotes. Mr. Jimmy claims that he singlehandedly reduced the administrative cost of the government by fifty percent, that he saved the citizens of Georgia $50 million a year, and that he left office with a $200 million surplus in the treasury. A closer look at the record reveals that Mr. C. is no David, slinging pebbles at a bloated bureaucracy; what he is throwing has a much stronger odor. Consider:

• During Carter's tenure as governor, the state budget rose from $1.06 billion to over $1.68 billion — a fifty-nine percent increase in less than four years.

• During the same period, *no* state jobs were eliminated. In fact, the number of employees jumped from 49,000 to 60,000. And the number of state employees drawing salaries of $20,000 or more annually was three times higher when he left office than when he entered the governor's mansion.

• During just the first year of his reorganization program, the Georgia budget increased $343 million — a higher leap than the *combined* total increase of the previous three years.

• The question of the alleged budget surplus leads to even murkier waters. In his autobiography, *Why Not The Best?*, Carter claims that he left office with a $200-million budget surplus. In campaign speeches in 1976, however, that figure had been trimmed to $116 million, with no explanation of what happened to the other $84 million.

However, even the $116 million figure is a fake. First, Carter *inherited* a surplus of $91 million. In the last fiscal year that he actually controlled the budget, the surplus had dipped to only $43 million — for a *loss* of $48 million. But wait, there's more. During that same period of time, the state's outstanding debt *increased* from $892 million to $1.097 billion — which means another $204 million was taken from the taxpayers' pockets.

Small wonder that State Auditor Ernest Davis admitted he could find no evidence that Carter's much-vaunted reorganization saved any money at all.

If this were the only instance where Carter's claims were poles apart from the facts, it would be enough to give every voter serious doubts about the validity of Carter's oft-repeated promise, "Trust me. I'll never lie to you." But in case after case that we investigated, we found that the Carter record contradicted the Carter rhetoric. Indeed, the Carter lies may be even more numerous than those little liver pills manufactured by a namesake.

"I achieved welfare reform by opening up 136 day-care centers for the retarded and using welfare mothers to staff them," Carter told a rapt audience in Mississippi one night in 1976. "Instead of being on welfare, these thousands of women now have jobs and self-respect. You should see them bathing and feeding the retarded children. They're the best workers we have in the state government."

It sounds magnificent. The blue-collar workers and wives who heard him were blinking back tears. *The New York Times Magazine* picked up the story and went into raptures of ecstasy over it.

There was just one problem with the glorious image Carter concocted: it was pure fantasy. Derril Gay, deputy director of the state Mental Health Division, acknowledged that *not a single welfare mother in Georgia* had a job in a day-care center. Oh, well.

Jody Powell, the Carter press secretary (who is not

above playing fast and loose with the truth himself), admitted there was no such program, adding only that "if Carter mentioned such a program, I guess he was mistaken." One reporter who travelled with the candidate comments wryly: "While I accompanied him, he made the mistake before five audiences in three days." Ah, yes, there seems to be a little bit of blarney in the Carter peanut butter.

As we noted earlier, one of the minor issues of Carter's successful campaign against Carl Sanders concerned Georgia's "right-to-work" law. Under Section 14(b) of the Taft-Hartley Act, states were given the right to pass legislation preventing unions from *requiring* an employee to join a union to get a job in a "union" shop.

Carter warned the independent-minded workers of Georgia that Sanders would *repeal* Georgia's right-to-work law. If you want to remain free to decide for yourself, Carter told them, support me. On January 19, 1971, in fact, Governor Carter sent a letter on official stationery to the National Right To Work Committee, declaring: "I stated during my campaign that I was not in favor of doing away with the right-to-work law, and that is a position I still maintain."

Fine. That seems clear enough. But by the middle of his term — with his eye already on the White House — Jimmy had changed his tune. In 1973 he was telling labor representatives that *if* the Georgia Legislature passed a bill repealing the state's right-to-work law, he would be happy to sign it. However, he added firmly, the *state* should make that decision, not the federal government — clearly indicating that he opposed a *federal* repeal of Section 14(b).

What about today? Jimmy Carter has traveled a lot further along the road to Washington; and Big Labor is a lot more important to a Democratic nominee for

President than it is to an incumbent governor in Georgia who can't succeed himself. Mr. Peanut's message today is a bit different. "I think Section 14(b) should be repealed . . . . if the Congress passes such legislation, I'd be glad to sign it." And then he adds, "My position now is the same as in 1970, when I was running for governor."

We will be the first to admit a man can change his mind. Even two or three times. It could be just coincidence that every change occurred as Carter was taking another step up the ladder to political success. But when he switches direction three times, then says he has never moved at all, and promises in addition that he will never lie to us, something is definitely wrong. Either words have lost their meaning — or Jimmy Carter doesn't keep his word.

Jimmy Carter doesn't like bussing of school children, you understand. But after all, the Supreme Court is "the law of the land" and those federal judges must be obeyed.

Well, what about a constitutional amendment to ban court-ordered bussing? Jimmy is very clear; he opposes such an amendment, and has always opposed such an amendment.

But wait . . . back in 1972 Governor Carter urged Georgia parents to *support* a constitutional ban on bussing. In fact, he said that if the Georgia Legislature failed to pass a resolution favoring such an amendment, he would support a one-day boycott of the schools. Jimmy changed his mind again — but he says he never changed at all. To be charitable, maybe he just has an incredibly convenient memory.

If legislation isn't the answer to bussing, what is? Mr. C.'s favorite word here is "voluntarism." In fact, he says that as governor he "worked hard" on a voluntary bussing plan for Atlanta. But when syndicated columnists

Evans and Novak investigated Carter's claim, they found: "Nobody in Atlanta, either with the school board or the NAACP, remembers Governor Carter working on the plan — 'hard' or otherwise . . . . 'For him to claim that he did anything to help a settlement is an outright lie,' one black leader told us." And *Esquire* magazine, which conducted its own check, elaborated on Jimmy's trickery: ". . . the feeling at the time was that Carter shrewdly avoided any identification with the whole business until it had been settled and seemed okay."

This, then, is the other side of the Carter record. It is not surprising that Reg Murphy, former editor of the *Atlanta Constitution*, describes Carter as "one of the four phoniest men I ever met." Former Governor Sanders says, "Carter is far more liberal than I ever was."

By the time his term ended, every candidate in the race to succeed him as governor worked hard to avoid being associated with Carter. When he left the governor's mansion in January 1975, the Georgia peanut farmer had so little popularity at home that his endorsement would do a candidate more harm than good.

Jimmy C. didn't mind. With a primary schedule in one hand and a toothbrush in the other, he was already moving far down the road from Plains, Georgia. The next time he stopped, it would be in the White House.

3 The Secret Strategy

Jimmy Carter's express train to the White House might have been built in Plains, Georgia; but it received its first fuel in Miami, Florida. It was at the Democratic National Convention in 1972 that Jimmy first discovered the intoxicating effects of national publicity, national politics, and national power. He learned to wheel and deal with the best of them.

Like every other rung Carter has climbed on the ladder to national stardom, Jimmy's activities before, during, and after the 1972 convention are the subject of considerable controversy. Perhaps no one knows the whole story; but there are an awful lot of persons who say Carter proved in Miami that he knew how to use the shoulders of others to reach new heights himself. And he didn't care who he stepped on.

The major figure from the South that year was of course Alabama's feisty Governor, George Wallace. Carter had ridden Wallace's coattails into the governor's mansion in Georgia, and Wallace says he had a firm commitment from his neighbor to support his own candidacy. Wallace is unequivocal that Carter pledged to endorse him if Wallace entered the convention with at least 300 delegates; despite his physical infirmity, Wallace had won more than 400 votes.

To demonstrate a "united front" from the South, Wallace asked the relatively unknown governor from

Georgia to second the Alabamian's nomination for President. But by this time, Carter had received a better offer: He had a chance to deliver the *nominating* speech for Senator Henry Jackson of Washington. Ol' George was left muttering in the dust.

At one point during the 1976 campaign, Carter angrily denied that he had ever been asked to second Wallace's nomination. Eventually, aides were forced to show him copies of correspondence *from his own files* confirming the request and his rejection. There's that convenient memory again.

Jackson's candidacy in 1972 never really had a chance. And by 1976 Carter was saying that he was, after all, not that hot about the Senator from Washington anyway; he found Jackson's "exploitation" of bussing "disgusting;" "As I've learned more about him," Carter intoned piously, "I don't feel so close to him anymore." Sanford Ungar, writing in the July 1976 issue of *The Atlantic*, says that, "The change of heart seems to date roughly from the fall of 1972, when Jimmy Carter decided he would like to try to become President himself."

Up until the moment when George McGovern's nomination was confirmed, Jimmy Carter was part of the "Stop McGovern" forces at the Democratic Convention. But once the mad dove from South Dakota had captured the top rung on the roost, Carter wanted to become a chicken, not a chickenhawk, too. One of the first persons standing in the line for the number-two spot was Jimmy Carter! Julian Bond, the fiery black Democrat from Atlanta, says that on two occasions — before Thomas Eagleton was chosen and once again after he was dumped — Carter asked Bond to contact McGovern on his behalf. McGovern aides say that Hamilton Jordan, now Carter's campaign manager, also made a pitch for a Carter vice presidency. And Andrew Young, perhaps Carter's staunchest supporter among blacks, says he was aware in 1972 that Bond was asked to approach McGovern.

Now, however, the Goober King flatly denies making any such overtures. Bond — who supported Carter in the early stages of the peanut farmer's campaign for the presidency, but doesn't anymore — says flatly, "Carter lies."

While the Jimmy shuffle at the convention didn't endear the Georgia governor to Wallace, Jackson, or McGovern, there was one investment the wily strategist made in Miami that paid off in spades four years later. He opposed the McGovernites' move to throw Richard Daley and "the Daley machine" out of the convention. Carter lost the vote but won the war. Four years later, a beaming Mayor Daley threw his Illinois voting block behind Carter at a crucial time in the campaign, and helped trigger the avalanche that wiped out every other candidate.

Carter emerged from the mobocratic mess in Miami with exactly what he wanted: his nominating speech for Jackson had gained him national publicity; he made some powerful friends behind the scenes; and he was recognized as a "comer" among the political pros. No matter that he ruffled a few feathers in the process; Jimmy knew better than anyone else that *everybody* loves a winner. And by the fall of 1972, he knew exactly how he was going to collect the grandest prize in American politics.

Carter left Miami convinced that the Democratic standard bearer in 1972 was a loser. By the time the voters confirmed his appraisal in November, giving Nixon more electoral votes than any other candidate in history, the peanut planter was getting ready to make sure that the party would have a winner four years later. And the best candidate he could find was . . . himself.

The summer studies and strategy sessions had been reduced, by the fall of 1972, to a seventy-page outline for the forthcoming campaign. The two whiz kids who planned the program were Jody Powell and Hamilton Jordan.

Powell has been Carter's press secretary since Jimmy became governor. He knows his boss so well, according to *U.S. News & World Report*, that "he can just about anticipate what the former Governor wants to say." But Powell seems a curious choice, to say the least, to be Carter's alter ego with the media. Since very few reporters intentionally antagonize a future President, there has been an understandable reluctance to question Carter about the propriety of having, as press secretary, a chain-smoking, heavy-drinking PR man who was kicked out of the Air Force Academy for cheating. Powell, who is as disheveled as Carter is neat, is known for a lack of tact and a bristling devotion to his man. The hot-tempered press secretary once replied to a prominent Augusta matron, who had castigated the governor for his equivocation on bussing, with a letter which concluded: "I respectfully suggest that you take two running jumps and go straight to hell." During the 1976 campaign, Powell ended a conversation with a persistent reporter with the inelegant but explicit, "Up yours."

He was equally arrogant with me at the convention, when I had the unmitigated gall to ask some tough questions about Carter's patrons from the world of oil.

Most of the press has learned that, to get along with Carter, you must go along with Powell. One of the few journalists who dared cross swords with him is Lewis H. Lapham, editor of *Harper's* magazine. In January 1976,

Powell learned that *Harper's* was going to publish an article in its March issue that would be critical of Carter. He called Lapham on January 30 and asked to see an advance copy. The *Harper's* editor describes what happened next:

> *I explained that the text of the article would not become generally available for about three weeks, and asked Powell not to distribute any copies of it. Yes, sir, he said, on my word of honor. That was Friday afternoon. I hadn't yet read in* Time *magazine that Powell had been expelled from the Air Force Academy for cheating on a history examination, and I did not yet appreciate his indifference to the meaning of language.*
>
> *On the following Monday, February 2, Powell distributed photocopies of the article to reporters friendly to Carter.*

But the topper for Lapham was that three days later the candidate himself went before the television cameras to denouce the "very, very vicious" article — and to protest loud and long that *Harper's* had been so despicable that it had made sure the piece was "widely distributed" in advance. "At that time," Lapham notes, "*the only copies of the magazine that had been distributed were those distributed by Jody Powell.*"

But the most significant aspect of the whole stormy debate over the article was that no reporters from the major media commended the author, Steven Brill, for digging out some important facts that had been deliberately suppressed by the Carter camp. Instead, almost to a man they attacked the author, the editor, and the magazine. *The New York Times* correspondent assigned to the Carter campaign, Christopher Lydon, asked Brill: "How could you do such a thing? He's the only good guy we've got." ("We've got"? How's that for objective reporting from the world's most influential newspaper?)

Perhaps the significance of all this has been exaggerated. But it gives one pause to realize, as columnist William Safire has pointed out, that it will be Jody Powell who "would be in charge of never lying to us as press secretary."

Hamilton Jordan, who is cool where Powell is hot, softspoken where Powell is loud and profane, was the original author of the Carter campaign strategy. An avowed atheist, he was appointed by Carter as his executive secretary in 1970, when Carter took office as Governor, and is now Jimmy's national campaign manager.

The strategy Jordan outlined in the fall of 1972 consisted of four basic steps:

1. The first year, 1973, was to be spent learning about the issues, and starting a program to get the country learning about the governor. (Jordan suggested that Carter begin at once reading the *New York Times* every day, to get a better understanding of national issues and events. Carter agreed.)

2. During 1974 (his last year as governor), Carter was to become intimately involved in Democratic Party affairs, traveling as much as possible around the country. This goal was fulfilled beyond Jordan's wildest dreams when, at the Democratic Governors Conference in the spring of 1973, Carter approached party chairman Robert Strauss and offered to head the Democratic National Committee's campaign committee the next year. Strauss apparently had no idea he was being set up and agreed. Jordan (who called the coup the "Trojan peanut" operation) went to Washington to direct the committee staff, and Carter, in the word's of *U.S. News*,

had secured "an almost priceless opportunity to gather political intelligence and run up political IOUs."

3. The candidate and his family would travel almost non-stop in 1975, setting up field organizations and preparing for the delegate-selection process in 1976. So detailed was the planning that, in December 1974, Carter said that his entire schedule for the next year had already been planned down to the day.

4. The acid test for the Jordan projection would come during the first three months of 1976. The nomination would be won in the primaries and state caucuses, not at a brokered convention, Jordan contended. If Carter could lead the pack in the Iowa caucus in January, win the first-in-the-nation New Hampshire primary in February, and then knock off George Wallace in the Florida primary in March, he could build up a momentum that would carry him right through the convention.

That is exactly what occurred.

The Jordan document was meticulously researched and brilliantly organized. But the most important aspect of the entire strategy was Jordan's realization, back in 1972, that the nation was tired of controversy, tired of divisiveness, tired of issues. Personalities and emotions would determine our next President, he argued, not a candidate's platform or political positions. And Jimmy Carter was just the man to carry such a strategy to victory.*

On January 14, 1975, when Jimmy Carter walked out of the governor's mansion and began his full-time cam-

---

* Ray Abernathy, who worked on Carter's 1970 campaign, agreed completely. "He has an ability, in public, to be warm, personable. In private, he can be cold, hard, even ruthless. Precise. Demanding. He has that ability to change. He's a dream candidate, a perfect politician." Not quite the image the Carter campaign has created, but *exactly* what Jordan said it would take to win.

paign for the presidency, he did not have many old cronies to call on for help. His fellow Democratic governors shunned him almost to a man, until it became obvious that he had the nomination all wrapped up. He was not popular at the governors' conferences he had attended; according to *Los Angeles Times* political writer Bill Boyarsky, "He was a poor mixer and was always hustling for publicity."

Wendell Ford, former Governor of Kentucky, admitted in early 1976:

> *I don't know of any governors or former governors whom Carter contacted for support. That might indicate how much support he has among his former colleagues.*

And *Saga* magazine in July 1976 quotes a former governor of a Northern state as adding:

> *It was obvious he was a hustler. His style was just a little bit different: soft voice, soft sell. But there was a political road map all over his face. Jimmy would take advantage of any single opportunity to further himself. He is absolutely driven. But unlike a lot of politicians, he knows who he is and where he wants to go.*

Yes, he knew where he wanted to go — an eight-year residency at 1600 Pennsylvania Avenue. And he knew the road to Washington wound through Iowa, Florida, New Hampshire, Michigan, and forty-six other states. Jimmy, the "driven" man, began campaigning with fervor.

The day after he left the governor's mansion, Jimmy Carter began an eighteen-hour-a-day, six-days-a-week, twelve-months-a-year quest for votes. He made 63 trips to Florida before the Democratic primary there. He visited 110 towns in Iowa in a caucus campaign likely to be written about in political science textbooks.

He won friends, and votes, by getting out earlier, and staying out later, than any other candidate. Once, shaking hands in a department store in Ohio, he grabbed the hand of a manikin by mistake. He was so intent on winning votes he never realized his error; he just smiled and smiled and told an aide, "Give her a brochure."

Over and over again, Carter delivered his evangelical message in his soft Southern drawl: "I'll never tell a lie. I'll never knowingly make a misstatement of fact. I'll never betray your trust. If I do any of these things, I don't want you to support me."

Even his most severe critics (and there are plenty of them — although for some strange reason they get almost no play in the media) acknowledge that Carter is a master at personal gatherings. He has a charisma that is strangely compelling; even veteran reporters confess being swept along by the Carter mystique.

Consider, for example, Carter's talk with a dozen teenagers in Jackson, Mississippi. The youths were the leaders of their respective high schools, and because Mississippi law allows seventeen-year-olds to vote in the delegate-selection caucus, their influence was considerable. Here is how the March 1976 issue of *Harper's* reported the event:

> *"I grow peanuts over in Georgia," Carter begins softly, his blue eyes finding each of them one by one. "I'm the first child in my daddy's family who ever had a chance." His voice is humble yet proud. "I used to get up at four in the morning to pick peanuts. Then I'd walk three miles along the railroad track to deliver them. My house had no running water or electricity . . . . But I made it to*

the U.S. Naval Academy and became a nuclear physicist . . . .

"Now I want to be your President, so I can give you a government that's honest and that's filled with love, competence, and compassion . . . . If you have any questions or advice for me, please write. Just put 'Jimmy Carter, Plains, Georgia' on the envelope, and I'll get it. I open every letter myself and read them all."

And then came the close. It had been delivered a thousand times before, but it still sounded fresh, spontaneous, and totally sincere:

"One more thing," he continues, his voice starting to quiver. "If I ever lie to you" — his voice drops off; he waits about three seconds — "or if I ever mislead you" — two more seconds — "please don't vote for me."

On paper it may sound schmaltzy. But in person it is incredibly effective; it would take an incurable cynic to remember the reaction of Ralph Waldo Emerson to a similar appeal: "The more he spoke of his honor, the faster we counted our spoons."

It came as an incredible shock to the reporter covering that Carter talk to learn, a day or two later, that Jimmy *never* sees any mail addressed to him in Plains, Georgia. It is forwarded automatically to Carter headquarters in Atlanta, where it is opened, processed, recorded, and answered by high-speed computer equipment.

The most charitable thing any honest reporter can say is that Carter fudges. He gilds the lily. He elaborates and fabricates. He stretches, bends, and twists the facts. *He lies.*

Carter is not, as he has claimed, a nuclear physicist.

He has a Bachelor's degree from Annapolis and took a few post-graduate courses — hardly enough to qualify him for a Ph.D. He is not "a farmer." The family enterprise is primarily a middleman operation — warehousing, buying, and shelling peanuts along with selling fertilizer, herbicides, and seeds. Moreover, Carter has not held a fulltime position with the firm for fourteen years. He is *not* just a small businessman — he is well on his way to becoming a millionaire, and his investments pay off so handsomely that he nets nearly $50,000 a year from them.

. Nor was his childhood as deprived as he would have us believe — especially in comparison to the lives of his peers in Depression-stricken southern Georgia. His own mother, the outspoken Miss Lillian, has said:

> *I know Jimmy writes about how poor we were, but really, we were never poor . . . . In fact, while Jimmy was growing up, we had all the help I wanted. I had a cook for one dollar a week, and another girl worked for us from the time she was thirteen and made fifty cents a week.*
>
> *We weren't poor . . . . We always had a car. We had the first radio in Plains. We had the first TV set.*

A cook for one dollar a week? A thirteen-year-old servant girl for fifty cents a week? The only things lacking are mint juleps on the veranda and Aunt Jemima waving dem flies away.

It is obvious that Carter employs a bit of "poetic license" once in a while. But when his "exaggerations" are found out, he is not very gracious about conceding his error. As Thomas W. Ottenad of the *St. Louis Post-Dispatch* has observed:

> *When caught up in contradictions or inconsisten-*

cies, Carter does not yield easily. He tends to explain that his staff did not follow up or that an aide wrote a letter which Carter did not see or that Carter had forgotten an incident from the past or that he was unaware of some tactic in his campaign.

Ottenad then cites this revealing example:

In New Hampshire he once denied to reporters that his campaign was using a tough radio commercial blaming his Presidential rivals for the country's tax problems. The commercial, it turned out, included Carter's own voice. Although he told reporters indignantly that he might kill the spot announcement, it remained on the air until election day, and a similar spot was used in the Florida campaign two weeks later.

What kind of man will look a group of teenagers in the eye, swear by all that's Holy he will never lie to them, and then *lie* to them? What sort of person is this, who will knowingly mislead a group of reporters — trusting that the truth will not be discovered — and then lie about the original falsehood? Is Jimmy Carter, as *The Review of the News* has contended, "a compulsive liar"? Does he have one hand on the Bible, but the other behind his back with the fingers crossed? Or is he simply one of the most ruthless, ambitious, egotistical, and amoral politicians of this century? Is he *that* "driven"?

Responsible journalists who have looked to Jimmy's religious convictions, hoping to find an answer to the puzzling enigma of Jimmy Carter, have remained confused and uncertain.

The subject of Carter's religion has been raised frequently during the 1976 Presidential primaries — quite often because Jimmy himself has initiated, or at least encouraged, such discussion. It is a subject that makes most commentators somewhat uneasy; in part because a man's relationship with God is such an intensely personal matter, and in part because the need for the separation of church and state is deeply ingrained in all of us.

Jimmy Carter's religious convictions are as puzzling as the strange dichotomy between his words and his deeds in the political arena. He is a "born-again" Christian whose favorite theologian is the ultra-modernist Reinhold Niebuhr, former professor at Union Theological Seminary, who was a founder of Americans for Democratic Action, had a list of Communist-front affiliations as long as your arm, and who openly derided "born-again" believers. Niebuhr denied the inerrancy of the Bible, the Divine conception of Christ, His virgin birth, and His bodily resurrection as the Son of God. For Carter to call himself a "born-again believer" whose favorite theologian is Reinhold Niebuhr is like a rabbi saying his favorite politician is Hitler.

Carter says that his relationship with God is the most important factor of his life; but when asked by his evangelist sister, Ruth Carter Stapleton, if he would give up politics for Christ, he answered "no."

Carter has been extremely active in his Southern Baptist church since he joined at the age of ten. He was a Sunday School teacher when he was sixteen and a deacon in his twenties. And yet he says he was not "born-again" until 1967 — more than thirty years after becoming a local Christian leader. Carter does not accept the inerrancy of the Bible — a basic doctrine of Southern Baptists. He has given up drinking hard liquor during the campaign for political, not religious, reasons. He is, emphatically, not a fundamentalist.

In a special one-hour appearance on *Meet the Press* the day before the Democratic Convention began,

Carter said the question of his religion had created some problems in his campaign. "I had a hard time deciding whether to respond truthfully to questions about my religion," he admitted. But when honesty is a calculated policy, it is *not* a principle. It was an extremely pragmatic statement for a man whose life, we are told, is wholeheartedly surrendered to Christ.

Quite often, in fact, political considerations seem to override Carter's personal convictions. Columnist Jack Anderson quoted one source close to Carter as saying, "When Jimmy Carter talks about the Catholic bloc or the Jewish bloc, he is interested in their votes, not their souls." But the primary concern of "born-again" Christians, second only to their relationship with God, should be the lost sheep who will be condemned to Hell for eternity without a saving knowledge of Jesus Christ.

Speechwriter Robert Shrum, who defected from the Carter camp nine days after going to work for the Democratic nominee, has said that the double-talk, half-truths, and blatant hypocrisy of the man were too much for him to swallow. Shrum quotes the following orders from the boss as one of the reasons he got off an obviously winning bandwagon:

> *"Don't send me any more statements on the Middle East or Lebanon. Jackson has all the Jews anyway." His tone was hard; the anger broke through his normal monotone. "It doesn't matter how far I go. I don't get over 4 percent of the Jewish vote anyway, so forget it. We get the Christians."*

Wow! Is Carter saying the Christians could be had? The same disturbing questions arise concerning Carter's autobiography, *Why Not The Best?* The book, which was admittedly written to boost Carter's candidacy, was published by the Broadman Press, a division of the Southern Baptist Convention's Sunday School Board. And yet the book is strangely muted in its discussion of religion; there are none of the appeals to "accept Christ" one expects in a Baptist publication. It reads like what it is — a political appeal.

Thus, it was unusual, to say the least, to have a Baptist religious organization financing extensive advertising for the book in the Bible Belt of the South — just when Jimmy's campaign was getting underway.

When a Christian publisher promotes the autobiography of a Presidential candidate as "must reading in this campaign year," it is awfully hard not to believe that Jimmy Carter has deliberately mixed religion and politics — to his own advantage. He knew *exactly* what he was doing when he gave his church publishers a book that would become a campaign document; and he is surely aware that major advertisements for the book — and thus for him — are being paid for by a subdivision of the Southern Baptist Convention. Or could it be that the folks at Broadman's were had?

We do not mean to infer that Carter has done anything legally or even morally wrong. It is simply that when a man wears his religion on his sleeve, as well as in his heart, he is inviting close scrutiny. And the closer we look, the more questions that arise. If the press were not telling us, over and over again, that he is not just another politician, we would begin to suspect that he is.

But whatever his methods, and whatever his motives, there is no doubt that the peanut farmer from Plains engineered "the miracle campaign" of the 1970s.

4 The Miracle Campaign

On December 12, 1974 former Governor James Earl Carter, Jr. of Georgia announced that he planned to seek the Democratic nomination for President of the United States. The newspapers in Atlanta laughed; the media in other areas ignored the story.

After one full year of active campaigning, the Gallup Poll reported in December 1975 — only seven months before the nominating convention — that less than four percent of Democrats nationwide wanted Jimmy Carter as their standard bearer in 1976. Carter trailed Hubert Humphrey, Henry Jackson, Edmund Muskie, Birch Bayh, Ted Kennedy, and even George Wallace and George McGovern in the polls. His name was down at the bottom among the "others" — such stalwarts as Sargent Shriver, Fred Harris, Milton Shapp, and Terry Sanford.

Six months later the peanut politico with the dazzling dentures had the nomination sewed up. Psychic Jeanne Dixon predicted he would be the next President, London bookmakers reported that bets totalling $200,000 had been placed on the peanut king winning the big apple, and the Carter campaign staff considered telling all the politicians showing up in Plains to jump on the bandwagon, "Take a number please; we'll see you as soon as possible."

Carter had entered thirty state primaries and won

nineteen of them; his next-closest competitor was the leader in only four. To judge by the hosannas and hoopla in the national media, verily a political miracle had occurred. And yet . . .

While the boys on the bandwagon have convinced almost the entire electorate that Carter was the overwhelming choice of the Democrats, the truth is that only 4.3 percent of the nation's eligible voters had marked their ballots for him. Forty percent of the states did not have a primary at all; in the thirty-one that did, Carter won a majority of primary votes in only five of them.

But if the common man in America had not stood up, one-hundred-million strong, and called out "Jimmy, Jimmy, Jimmy" in one loud voice, what did happen? The undeniable truth is that, during the first six months of 1976, we witnessed one of the slickest, most intensive, most professional media campaigns in history. Since the show was free, and we didn't even need a ticket for it, most watchers weren't aware that the whole thing was a staged performance.

We've commented before on the slippery trick at *Time*, when cover artists were ordered to make Carter look as much like Kennedy as possible. But that was just for starters. Early in the campaign, *Time* produced a full-page ad, ostensibly promoting the magazine's political coverage, that looked — and read — as though it were prepared by a Carter ad agency. A flattering photo of the candidate took half the space; a huge headline puffing Jimmy filled the top; a persistent reader had to look at the small print on the bottom to learn it was an ad for *Time*, not for Mr. Smiley Sunshine himself.

Time ran copies of the ad in the following publications during the six weeks prior to the New Hampshire primary: *People, Sports Illustrated, Forbes, Harper's, The Atlantic, Psychology Today, The Smithsonian, Atlanta, Chicago, Cleveland, Harvard Business Review, Los Angeles, the National Observer, New Times, San Francisco,* and *Texas Monthly.* Even Nelson Rockefeller would be hard pressed to *buy* that kind of publicity. And it didn't cost Carter a single peanut.

Or consider this story from the *Los Angeles Times,* the most widely read newspaper in the western states. It started with thirty column inches on the front page, and continued for nearly one-quarter of a page on the inside. The opening paragraphs sounded like a movie script for Charlton Heston:

> *Lightning flashed over Philadelphia and thunder rolled, but neither the gloom of the day nor the violence of the storm could dim the smile of Jimmy Carter.*
>
> *It came flashing through the downpour like a neon sign blinking "Win" off and on, and when he reached the protective overhang of a large building, he shook the nearest hand and said, "How y'all" in the drowsy voice of a sunny Georgia morning.*
>
> *The contradiction was perfect, and those he greeted on that wet and roaring afternoon could not help but be impressed by the tousle-haired man striding through the rain, grinning.*
>
> *"He seems," a spectator said, watching him, "somehow drier than everyone else."*

With coverage like this from coast to coast, is it any wonder that mere mortals got left far, far behind? The way Carter was hyped by the national media, most voters would not have been surprised to learn that he had parted the waters of Lake Erie on his way to Detroit.

Granted, as Richard Strout commented in the

Christian Science Monitor, that Jimmy Carter "skillfully grabbed the great salivating American publicity media machine for his 'product.' " Those good ol' boys in Atlanta who did a number on Carl Sanders four years earlier wanted to prove they could be positive, too. Jerry Rafshoon, a successful Atlanta advertising executive who has handled Carter's commercials since 1972, knew how the game was played. He got Jimmy dressed up in denims and had some *great* pictures shot of his boss shoveling peanuts. And suddenly, in virtually every supermarket in America, there was Jimmy in *People* magazine, aworkin' away in the noonday sun. You could almost hear the housewives sigh, "That's *my* kind of man."

Rafshoon freely admits the picture was "a phony." But that's the way it's done, boys. Rafshoon even used the same image in a commercial he produced; the voice-over asks, "Can you imagine any other candidate working in the hot August sun?" No, we can't. And we can't imagine Carter doing it either — unless it's to get his picture in the papers.*

And when it came to appealing to special interest groups, the Carters had no match. There was son Jeff, telling youthful voters that he had tried marijuana and felt "it should be legalized and sold openly." (Dad didn't go that far; he would only say that it should be "decriminalized.") Son Chip flew out to San Francisco to enter a "gay tricycle race," staged to gain attention for the "gay people's political situation." Chip broke his handlebars and didn't finish in the money. But he was

---

* Rafshoon's talents so impressed the state Board of Community Development in Georgia — whose members were appointed by Governor Carter — that in 1973 his agency received an annual contract of $750,000 to promote Georgia tourism. Rafshoon's fee in the deal, which runs through 1977, is $108,000 a year.

able to get his message across: His father "doesn't think homosexuality is right, but doesn't want to inflict his morals on other people."

For all those television viewers who thought *Star Trek* was for real, there was an exclusive article in the *National Enquirer*, with headlines on the cover three inches high: JIMMY CARTER: THE NIGHT I SAW A UFO. Addressing a group of rabid women's libbers in New Jersey, there was Rosalynn Carter wearing her Medallion of Honor from NOW — the ultra-radical National Organization of Women. Addressing a record manufacturers' convention in Florida, Carter praised the "acid-rock" group Led Zeppelin for helping to "expand his consciousness." Carter reminded the teeny-boppers (their parents can vote) that "My friend" Bob Dylan had actually been a guest in the governor's mansion.

The only time the well-oiled Carter machine slipped a gear was when Carter remarked, during an interview with the *New York Daily News*, that he saw nothing wrong with various groups "trying to maintain the ethnic purity of their neighborhoods." The civil rights crusaders and the liberal press were on him in a flash. It's a "Hitlerian" term, Carter's own premier black advocate, Rep. Andrew Young, declared, and demanded that Jimmy apologize at once.

Jimmy did better than that. He staged a rally in Atlanta's Central City Park; he reminded his audience of his oft-repeated statement, "The Civil Rights Act was the best thing that ever happened to the South." He proudly declared, "I would not be where I am if it were not for Martin Luther King, Jr." He shared parts of his "I-have-a-vision" speech, delivered with the same rolling cadences that King used in his "I-have-a-dream" talk.

Sharing the platform with him that afternoon was the

venerable Martin Luther King, Sr. And while the crowd shouted and wept, and voices in the background sang "We Shall Overcome," King and Carter embraced and exchanged a soul-brother handclasp. It was *some* apology.

As *Forbes* magazine editorialized the following month:

> *Fervent reassurances to the black community and embraces from Martin Luther King's father restore Jimmy's Black Magic.*
>
> *And the Silent Whites (who'd never speak of their worry about mixing their neighborhoods and schools) join the rednecks in concluding that Jimmy really shares their fears, but for political reasons has to back off from words that express his real feelings.*
>
> *Now who else could have turned apparent disaster into a voting harvest at the ensuing primary?*
>
> *Absolutely amazing, isn't it?*

Was that the ghost of Franklin Delano Roosevelt, who said "In politics there is no such thing as coincidence," that just winked? At the very least, Carter has a remarkable facility for turning the sourest lemons into the sweetest lemonade.

The Carter campaign was a masterpiece of brilliant strategy and faultless execution. It was put together by the relatively small palace guard that Carter had carefully assembled over the years — joined by a huge convoy of former campaigners for George McGovern and the Kennedys. In addition to Jordan, Powell, and Rafshoon, there was McGovern's former campaign manager, Frank Mankiewicz; former Kennedy aide Theodore Sorenson; pollster Patrick Caddell, who gained national attention for his work for McGovern four years earlier; Martin Luther King's former colleague in starting riots, Andrew Young; chief fundraiser Morris Dees, an attorney who is the darling of the far, far Left since he helped win an acquittal for Joan Little, a black convict in North Carolina who became a *cause celebre* for the Communist Party when she murdered a white jailer who allegedly raped her; Harold Willens, national chairman of Businessmen for Peace in Vietnam and western finance chairman for McGovern; Chris Brown, an organizer for Eugene McCarthy in 1968 and McGovern in 1972; and literally scores of other political pros from the left edge of the political spectrum.

The most amazing thing about a list of Carter campaign aides and organizers is that even with such a team, he has managed to convince a majority of voters that he is a conservative.

There is only one other ingredient that was necessary to complete the package: the money to finance the show. And if there is one question that is sure to raise the ire of the Carter camp, it is the simple inquiry, "Where did the funds come from *before* Jimmy became an overnight sensation?"

Syndicated columnist Ray Cromley reports:

> *The men and women within this closed group, and apparently Carter himself, resent too much prying into Carter's past activities, backers, and past money sources.*

A current list of Carter contributors reads like a "Who's Who" of the Establishment. The names range from Michael Taylor, vice president of Paine, Webber, Jackson & Curtis to Max Palevsky, the maverick multimillionaire who contributed $320,000 to McGovern's losing cause in 1972.

But it is the incomplete, fragmented list of *early* contributors — the men who put up the "seed money" so Jimmy Carter could become a winner — that might produce the most surprises. We have not been able to verify more than a handful of names from that select group. There were the expected donations from the Carter family itself and several thousand dollars from the Carter campaign treasurer, Robert J. Lipshutz. But there were some surprises, too:

• Henry Luce, vice president of Time, Inc. (Perhaps that explains the extraordinary publicity by the magazine conglomerate on behalf of J.C.)

• C. Douglas Dillon, former Secretary of the Treasury and a key figure in the inner circle of international bankers.

• Dean Rusk, former Secretary of State and a political insider for more than three decades.

• Cyrus Eaton, the avidly pro-Soviet industrialist who received the Lenin Peace Prize for his efforts on behalf of Moscow (and who is now teamed with the Rockefellers to promote "trade" to the Soviet bloc).

That's an unusual crop to come up in anybody's peanut patch! If deeds speak louder than words, it is even more true that "the man who pays the piper calls the tune." With contributors like Luce, Dillon, Rusk, and Eaton, the evidence is overwhelming that the peanut politico is *not* the simple, down-home boy he's cracked up to be.

All was not taters and grits throughout the grueling period of primaries. But Jimmy Carter proved the truth of that old adage, "When the going gets tough, the tough get profane." Told one night that Senator Ted Kennedy of Massachusetts had been mildly critical of the Georgia peanut king for not being more specific on the issues, Mr. Clean replied, "I don't have to kiss his ass." When he learned that Governor Jerry Brown of California had entered the race, in a last-ditch effort to stop his candidacy, the born-again Baptist "used expletives which I didn't know he knew," a supporter said.

The national press, too, began to detect a harsh edge to the Carter sword that was sweeping the country. One member of the Carter team, who had tried to offer some constructive criticism to The Candidate, retired to nurse his wounds after learning: "He is a very tough fellow. He seems to nurse grudges and he tends to lash out at people who criticize him, even when their intentions are purely honorable."

Vivian Gornick in *The Village Voice* commented on a phenomenon that every reporter travelling with Carter had observed on more than one occasion: When a writer pressed for an *answer*, instead of Mr. Peanut's usual mumbo-jumbo, "Slowly, the smile on Carter's face hardened, the features began to freeze, and the blankness in his eyes was crowded out by an American-blue ice that was truly frightening to look upon." Time and time again, even journalists who supported Smilin' Jim would observe that "his brilliant smile never really reached his eyes."

Joseph Kraft worried about "a streak of ugly meanness — an egotistical disposition to run right over people." Muckraking columnist Jack Anderson, author of what is probably the most widely read political column in America, observed that Carter "has acquired a palace guard before he has the palace." And he added, "There is a disgruntlement, too, about a Carter mean streak beneath the surface amiability, a hardness beneath the engaging sincerity, a political purpose behind the Billy Graham sermonettes."

Carter, the candidate who was probably the quickest to sense what pleased and displeased the press, moved earth (and may have asked heaven to shift, too) in his efforts to satisfy the media. His desire to curry favor with the reporters covering his campaign was as calculated as everything else he did. Early in the campaign, for example, he told his eight-year-old daughter Amy that she was not charging enough at her lemonade stand in Plains, Georgia. "These fellows are all on expense accounts and can afford a little bit more," he was heard to explain.

But, when Amy raised her prices (tuna fish sandwiches, $1.00) and reporters complained, Jimmy publicly rebuked his daughter for being a price-gouger: "Even fifty cents is too much for Plains," he said.

While the Carter mask may have slipped occasionally, the Carter confidence remained unchanged and unchallenged. As much as three months before the Democratic Convention, Rosalynn Carter was telling listeners how she planned to redecorate the White House. (One of Carter's top aides said, "She wants to be First Lady as much as he wants to be President." After a pause, he amended his comment: "No, she wants to be First Lady *more* than he wants to be President.") Jimmy, on his part, never said "*If* I am President . . . ." The operating word was always, "*When.*"

On the early days of the primary trail, the Carter candidacy was dismissed by most observers as an exercise in egotism. But by early June, Jimmy was the only one still smilin'. The Final Judgment came earlier than expected: Jimmy's victory in the Ohio primary on June 8 cinched his nomination.

The first to capitulate was George Wallace, who called his neighbor to the east at two o'clock in the morning to toss in the towel.* By the end of the day, Chicago's Mayor Richard Daley and Washington Senator Henry

---

* It was an ironic moment; as radio commentator Alan Stang observed, Carter had probably done more to wreck Wallace's Presidential ambitions than Arthur Bremer.

Jackson had both placed their delegates in the Carter basket; and even the ever-ready Hubert Humphrey conceded, "Governor Carter is virtually certain to be our party's nominee."

Carter then had more than a month to travel the country, accepting swords and collecting scalps. He didn't waste a minute of the time. And he had to be mighty pleased at such events as seeing 250 Democratic Congressmen standing in line in Washington, waiting to have their picture taken with him. Victory is indeed sweet, and to the victor go the spoils.

The national convention in New York in mid-July was an anti-climax. In his campaign autobiography, *Why Not The Best?*, Jimmy tells of his efforts, when he was about six years old, to sell bags of peanuts to people in his hometown:

> *I was able to distinguish very clearly between the good people and the bad people of Plains. The good people, I thought, were the ones who bought boiled peanuts from me!*

By Jimmy's criterion, the Democratic convention was filled with good people. They not only bought his peanuts, they bought the peanut vendor! The four-year Carter campaign, which cost a record $9 million, was over. Nominated by acclamation, Mr. Peanut was king of all he surveyed. And no one even checked what he was selling, to see if his product was as fresh and new as he claimed, or just another bag of wormy nuts.

5 Jimmy's "Efficient Socialism"

As Jimmy Carter's campaign for the Presidency progressed, more and more observers charged that the candidate's favorite food wasn't peanuts, but waffles. Mr. Clean could obfuscate more issues, with a talent for waffling that borders on genius, than most reporters believed possible. A *New York Times* survey of voters in Illinois, for example, found that Carter received the support of 47 percent of the voters who believe military spending should be reduced — and also 48 percent of those who say it should not be. Both sides said Carter was on their side.

Columnist William Rusher summed up the frustration of many journalists when he wrote:

Carter is a black-belt master of ambiguity. To read or hear one of his typical statements on a controversial issue is to discover entirely new possibilities for the English language as a means of non-communication: to be transported to realms where words, shorn at last of their semantic burden, pirouette and re-group in combinations hitherto undreamed of.

Typical of Carter's corkscrew approach to controversial topics has been his dazzling display of fancy footwork regarding the war in Vietnam. Two years ago, the governor flatly opposed amnesty for deserters and draft evaders. By mid-1976, however, Smilin' Jim was announcing that, "During my first week in office, I would issue a pardon to all Vietnamese defectors." We thought you were opposed to amnesty?, a reporter asked. "I am," J. C. replied. And then he invented new definitions for the two words, when he explained that "pardon" meant to drop charges, while "amnesty" meant the culprits were right. This will be news to the dictionary publishers of America, who had failed to notice such nuances in their previous editions.

It is a distinction without a difference, of course. And the radical agitators in the Fellowship of Reconciliation, SANE, Women Strike For Peace, the National Lawyers Guild, People's Party, American Civil Liberties Union, Women's International League for Peace and Freedom, War Resisters League, and the other pro-Communist groups that had demanded unconditional amnesty, were all delighted to accept Carter's definition of unconditional pardons.

Although as governor Jimmy was originally a fervent supporter of the American presence in Vietnam — going so far as to defend Lt. William Calley as a "scapegoat" and to proclaim American Fighting Men's Day in Georgia the day after Calley's conviction — by convention time 1976 he was an avid dove. Sounding more like Jane Fonda than a Presidential candidate, Carter even denounced Vietnam as "a racist war," and added that the U.S. would never have fire-bombed whites in Europe as it did yellow people in Indochina. Since Jimmy was a student at the U.S. Naval Academy at Annapolis in 1943-1946, he *must* have known about the British and American fire-bombings of almost every major German city. In just one raid on one day, for example, more than 240,000 white Europeans — most of them children, women, and old men — were burned to death in Dresden. Did the eight-year veteran of the military have a short memory? Or did he just hope his audience did?

It is this kind of waffling and weasling, combined with a gift for fuzziness and fudging, that has left so many voters so confused about Carter's stand on the issues. The problem is so real that an *Associated Press* national poll in June of this year disclosed:

> *Half of Jimmy Carter's supporters don't know where he stands on the issues, a quarter of them have the wrong idea of his positions, and only about 20 percent can correctly state his views . . . .*
>
> *The poll indicates a tendency for Carter supporters on both sides of an issue to think he agrees with them.*

The AP report went on to disclose that more than half of Carter's supporters admitted they didn't know where their man stood on the issues. Only 23 percent said they supported Carter because of his position on major issues — and even *this* group was wrong forty percent of the time, when asked to identify Carter's stand on five basic questions.

All of this is a terrible indictment of Carter's calculated confusion of the very critical issues confronting America. It is incredible that so few voters have been able to unravel Jimmy's amazing performance. And it is a shameful indictment of the cynicism and apathy of too many Americans that a majority will admit they don't even care where their candidate stands.

Jimmy has been purposefully vague and often contradictory about the issues, it is true. But it is *not* correct that his political plans are a mystery, wrapped in a puzzle, inside an enigma. A careful scrutiny of the record over the past six months does disclose a lot about the prospects of a Carter Administration. Most Carter supporters will be shocked to learn what their man really intends to do, once the reins of Presidential power are firmly in his grasp.

What follows is a brief summary of the Carter stand on some of the more important domestic issues facing America (foreign affairs will be discussed in the subsequent chapter). A reader who enjoys challenges is encouraged to review the bold-face headings, make a mental note of his own position, and then pick the position he *thinks* Carter favors, before reading the commentary that follows each item. You are in for some unpleasant surprises!

Abortion. Jimmy says that he personally opposes abortion. But he has refused any legislation that would protect an unborn child's right to life. In fact, he has even refused to oppose the federal funding of abortions.

Atomic power. Carter opposes the further development of peaceful uses of atomic energy, saying he would support it "only as a last resort." He favors internationalizing atomic power, and in a speech before a UN conference went so far as to propose that an almost-completed nuclear reprocessing plant in South Carolina be transferred to international control.

Education. Carter is in favor of a massive increase in federal spending — as much as $20 billion annually — for education. There should be "a rapid increase in the proportion of education costs to be financed by the federal government," he says. Which will not only mean higher taxes; it will also mean increased federal control of schools. Jimmy has been somewhat vague on how such funds would be spent — although one program he has already endorsed is nationwide sex education from kindergarten through college.

Federal aid to cities. "America's number one economic problem is our cities," Carter has said, and he promised unlimited federal funds to help solve it. Addressing the U.S. Conference of Mayors this June, he pledged: "I'll accept your demands as President . . . . I'll be there as a solid partner on which you can always depend." His program, he said, would mean "a restoration of federalism" — almost the *exact* words Nelson Rockefeller has used to describe his own socialist utopia under "a new federalism."

Government regulation. Carter is all in favor of it. He has said that the Occupational Safety and Health Administration should be strengthened, and he has promised to create a cabinet-level Consumer Protection Agency — a favored scheme of Ralph Nader.

Gun Control. Carter supports nationwide registration of handguns — the first step toward confiscation. Jimmy's chief fundraiser, Morris Dees, supports an effort that, he gloats, will "break the National Rifle Association" within five years.

Health Care. Carter has promised to enact "a nationwide, comprehensive, mandatory health-insurance program," to be financed by the federal government and by an employee-employer payroll tax, *a la* Social Security. The program would "guarantee to every citizen as a right as much care as he or she needs." The scheme would include federal controls over doctors' fees and hospital charges. Cost estimates for such socialized medical care range from $15 to $40 billion dollars a year.

Inflation. Like sin and big government, Carter says he is against it. But he has already declared that "an expansionary fiscal and monetary policy" will be necessary "to stimulate demand, production, and jobs." Translated, that means bigger deficits and more inflation.

Marijuana. Carter says he does not want to legalize it, but he does favor "decriminalization" — meaning that possession for personal use would not be a crime. Holding would be legal, baby.

Mass transit. "Operating subsidies for mass transit" are essential, Mr. C. believes.

Revenue Sharing. Both Carter's are in favor of it — the governor and the new candidate. They disagree, however, on *how* it should be shared. As governor, Carter had told the House Ways and Means Committee in 1971:

> *Cities and counties are creatures of the state. I do not favor any further fragmentation of Georgia people into isolated communities by unilateral agreements between local governments and Washington . . . bypassing the state would seriously undermine the state's authority and its ability to effectively serve the needs of all its people.*

By 1976, the "I'll-never-make-a-misstatement" candidate was saying:

> *. . . as I have proposed since I was governor of Georgia [sic], we need some change in the basic structure of dispersing revenue sharing funds. I would favor an approach which would give funds directly to local cities and communities rather than the states.*

By the time he is President, Honest Jim may have settled on the most efficient possible method of distribution of funds: simply mail a check to anyone who asks for one!

Unemployment. Carter has endorsed the Humphrey-Hawkins "full-employment" bill, which would *require* the federal government to create enough jobs to reduce unemployment to three percent. (If in effect today, that would mean four million public "make-work" jobs — at a cost of $12 to $40 billion annually.) The bill would also create machinery for bureaucratic "planning" of virtually every aspect of American economic life.

Wage and price controls. While Carter says that he would be reluctant to use them, he would ask Congress to grant him "standby controls which the President can apply selectively." In other words, here come de controls.

Welfare. Carter contends that ninety percent of the present recipients of welfare are unemployable, and he supports giving them "a uniform, nationwide payment to meet the basic necessities of life." (The few investigations of welfare fraud that have been made indicate that as many as half of the welfare payments may be going to cheaters.) Carter says the ten percent who are employable will be given training and found jobs by the federal government. No one has even tried to put a price tag on his welfare wonderland proposal.

Women's lib. Jimmy is an enthusiastic supporter of the radical Equal Rights Amendment; he blames "the John Birch Society and the textile mills" for causing its defeat in Georgia. The July 1976 issue of *Playgirl* magazine calls Jimmy their "feminist candidate" because "he has pledged to support virtually every issue of importance to the women's movement."

There you have it — a brief survey of how Jimmy Carter would make socialism acceptable. He has scored enormous points with voters, who love to hear him blast "the horrible, bloated, confused, overlapping, wasteful, insensitive, unmanageable, bureaucratic mess in Washington." But *nowhere* has he ever said he would reduce the massive size, spending, or power of the federal government.

The Carter platform is, in fact, tailor-made to bring socialism to America. And while the vast body of voters has no idea this is true, one group has seen through the pap being ground out for the masses to the lean Marxist meat on the inside. Three days after the amazing Mr. C. tied a bright-red bow around the Democratic convention, the Socialist Party of America (now marching under the more acceptable banner of Social Democrats USA) endorsed "the forward-thinking ticket" of Jimmy Carter and Walter Mondale. Indeed, so enthusiastic were the socialists by the Carter promise that they decided *against* running any national ticket this year — urging their members instead to campaign for the peanut politico.*

Time correspondent Stanley Cloud, who has covered the Carter campaign since before the New Hampshire primary, reveals: "As President, Carter would probably be far more liberal than many people now suspect." You ain't just whistling "Dixie," Stanley!

This June, *Human Events*, the conservative newsweekly from Washington, front-paged the story, "Carter Comes Out Of The Closet." The article began:

> With the Democratic nomination all but in his grasp, Jimmy Carter has started to come out of the closet. And contrary to all of the up-front advertising, he has done so in the gaudy plumage of big-spending Washington liberalism.
>
> Carter-as-collectivist-liberal is quite a switch from the image he tried to project throughout the primary season . . . .
>
> Carter has put his seal of approval on virtually every liberal boondoggle and social engineering scheme imaginable . . . . Where, in all of this, is

---

* The word about Carter's *real* intentions is obviously getting around. Former Chicago 7 defendant Tom Hayden told a CBS reporter that, while he himself didn't know much about the peanut vendor, his "close friends" say Honest Jim is "one hundred times more liberal than he appears to be." That's *almost* liberal enough to satisfy Mr. Jane Fonda.

there any glimmer of moderation, conservatism, or even ordinary common sense?

Few reporters for *any* publication have bothered to dig for the real facts about Carter's radical economic proposals. The media prefers to keep Carter's carefully contrived, anti-bureaucracy image brightly polished. One writer who was not fooled, however, was intelligence expert Frank A. Cappell, author of the weekly column, "An Intelligence Report," in *The Review of the News*.

And in his July 28 column, Cappell dropped a bombshell: Lawrence R. Klein, professor at the University of Pennsylvania's Wharton School of Business and Carter's *chief* economic adviser, was formerly a dues-paying member of the Communist Party, U.S.A. Cappell revealed that in 1954, under questioning by the House Committee on Un-American Activities, Klein admitted that he had taught at the Samuel Adams School in Boston (identified by Democratic Attorney General Tom Clark as "an adjunct of the Communist Party"); was on the staff of the Abraham Lincoln School in Chicago (cited as "a school to train Communist organizers and operatives" by the Senate Internal Security Subcommittee); and was, for a time, a Communist Party functionary who attended cell meetings and paid his dues promptly.

But here is the clincher: Klein said he left the Communist Party, not because he rejected Marxism, but because he found the meetings "too dull" and wanted to find a more effective way to promote Marxist socialism. When asked, 22 years ago, what that "better way" might be, Klein replied that many of his comrades believed the answer was to go to work for promising Democratic candidates!

Obviously, Klein has succeeded beyond his fondest

hopes. He is president-elect of the American Economic Association, a full professor at the prestigious Wharton School of Business, the number one economic adviser to the Democrats' Captain Marvel, and an almost-certain appointee to the President's Council of Economic Advisers, should Carter be elected. Not bad for a Red teacher who came in from the cold.

So if you have wondered why Carter's Economic Manifesto sounds like a southern-fried edition of the *Communist Manifesto*, you can stop looking for coincidences in the woodpile. An important termite planned it that way.

The Carter proposals listed above would add more than $100 billion a year to a federal budget already over $400 billion. We've had double-digit inflation in this country for years because Washington has been running in the red $1.5 billion *every week*. Jimmy Carter's schemes would more than double that deficit.

Pollster Lou Harris says his own sources among top Democrats admit that the Carter platform, if implemented, could nearly double the federal budget during his first term. Harris warned that federal spending could jump from the present stratospheric level of $400 billion a year to way beyond the ionosphere of $750 billion.

If even half of the Carter program is adopted, the average worker in America will face crippling new taxes, horrendous new regulations, and a spiraling rate of inflation that could wipe out any savings he hopes to have. It is a program for Big Government and "efficient socialism." It is enough to make any sensible person wring his hands in horror. But there is one group that is rubbing their hands in glee at the prospect.

6 The Un-Free Candidate

Nearly a month before the Democratic National Convention followed its predetermined course, Joseph C. Harsch, featured columnist for the *Christian Science Monitor*, laid down a line that would be dutifully echoed by other columnists and commentators in the national press:

> *[Carter] has that nomination without benefit of any single kingmaker, or of any power group or power lobby, or of any single segment of the American people. He truly is indebted to no one man and no group interest.*

Undoubtedly, most of Harsch's readers — in fact, most Americans — believe every word of it. One of the few persons who knew it was a clever fabrication was the author himself.

Harsch knew that Mr. Goober is owned, lock, stock, and peanut barrel, by the most powerful lobby in the country — the one organization that could truly claim to be kingmakers (and unmakers). The group is the Council on Foreign Relations, and Harsch is one of its members.

In a moment, we will document our charge that the Council on Foreign Relations, or, as it is generally called, the CFR, will be the real power behind the throne of a Carter Administration. But first some background information is necessary on this secretive combine — which

Harsch himself has described as "the true core of the so-called 'Eastern Establishment.' "

For more than fifty years, the CFR has operated like the Invisible Man in the novel by H. G. Wells. Its influence could be felt everywhere, but its actual existence was seldom seen.* The 1650 members of this elitist organization virtually dominate the fields of high finance, academics, politics, commerce, the foundations, and the communications media in this country. As John Franklin Campbell put it in *New York* magazine on September 20, 1971:

> *Practically every lawyer, banker, professor, general, journalist and bureaucrat who has had any influence on the foreign policy of the last six Presidents — from Franklin Roosevelt to Richard Nixon — has spent some time in the Harold Pratt House, a four-story mansion on the corner of Park Avenue and 68th Street, donated 26 years ago by Mr. Pratt's widow (an heir to the Standard Oil fortune) to the Council on Foreign Relations, Inc. . . . .*
>
> *If you can walk — or be carried — into the Pratt House, it usually means that you are a partner in an investment bank or law firm — with occasional "trouble-shooting" assignments in government. You believe in foreign aid, NATO, and a bipartisan foreign policy. You've been pretty much running things in this country for the last 25 years, and you know it. [Emphasis added]*

Just how powerful is the Council on Foreign Relations? Its membership includes top executives from

---

* In 1972, my own book exposing the Council of Foreign Relations, *None Dare Call It Conspiracy*, sold over 3 million copies — although the national media never even acknowledged its existence.

the *New York Times*, the *Washington Post*, the *Los Angeles Times*, the Knight newspaper chain, *NBC*, *CBS*, *Time*, *Fortune*, *Business Week*, *U. S. News & World Report*, and many others. If you have never heard of the CFR before, it is probably because the national media — which it controls — have planned it that way. (And if those same media decide to make a peanut farmer from Georgia an overnight political sensation, they can do that, too.)

CFR members control the big name foundations which expend more money and effort on politics than philanthropy; other members dominate the "best" colleges and universities; in the business community, there is scarcely a company in *Fortune*'s Top 100 that is not directed by a CFR member.

But the major influence of the Council on Foreign Relations is exercised in the most important *public* power center in the United States — the federal government in Washington, D.C. As Anthony Lukas commented in the *New York Times Magazine:*

> . . . *Everyone knows how fraternity brothers can help other brothers climb the ladder of life. If you want to make foreign policy, there's no better fraternity to belong to than the Council . . . .*
>
> *When Henry Stimson — the group's quintessential member — went to Washington in 1940 as Secretary of War, he took with him John McCloy, who was to become Assistant Secretary in charge of personnel. McCloy has recalled: "Whenever we needed a man we thumbed through the roll of the Council members and put through a call to New York."*
>
> *And over the years, the men McCloy called in turn called other Council members . . . . Of the first*

*82 names on a list prepared to help President
Kennedy staff his State Department, 63 were Council members . . . .*

The CFR provided the key men, particularly in the
field of foreign policy, for the Roosevelt, Truman,
Eisenhower, Kennedy, Johnson, Nixon, and now Ford
Administrations. Indeed, the man who is probably the
most powerful member of the Ford Administration (in-
cluding the President) is Henry Kissinger, who has
admitted that he was virtually "invented" by the CFR.*
And Vice President Nelson Rockefeller is not only a long-
time member of the CFR, his brother David is Chairman
of the Board of the group. The CFR has rightly been
called the "Shadow Government" or the "Invisible
Government" of the United States.

What is the goal of the Rockefellers' CFR? The
organization makes no bones about it. The CFR doesn't
have to disguise its ambitions because the media are not
about to excite the public with exposes of it. The
Rockefellers and the CFR call their "grand design" a
"New World Order." This is a phrase you will hear used
again and again by Rockefeller allies and hirelings.

"New World Order" is a CFR code phrase for a one-
world government. As John D. Rockefeller, Sr. learned so
well, when you control the government, you can control
the economy. The Rockefellers have been working for
five decades to control the American government so they
can dominate our economy.

But, most of the Rockefellers' wealth is located outside
the United States. The family has assets and does

---

* For the complete story of Kissinger's service to the CFR on behalf
of "a new world order," see the author's previous book, *Kissinger: The
Secret Side of the Secretary of State.* (1976: '76 Press, Seal Beach,
Calif.)

business in 125 separate countries. The Rockefeller game plan is to consolidate control over the world's economies by merging all the nations of the world under a single Rockefeller-controlled tent. Such a government would *have* to be a dictatorship, ruled by Rockefeller puppets or by the Communist-Third World bloc.

Since the Rockefellers' assets are spread across the globe, they long ago recognized the need to control U.S. foreign policy, regardless of whether the Republicans or the Democrats are in the White House. But to control policy, you must select the policy makers. This the Rockefeller-CFR combine has done for more than thirty years. Your only choice is between a Rockedem and a Rockepub foreign policy — whichever party is in power, the foreign policy decisions are always in the hands of dependable Rockefeller-CFR men.

What has all of this got to do with Jimmy Carter, that maverick politico from the deep South, who campaigned as a mortal enemy of the Eastern Establishment and the Washington bureaucracy?

It has *everything* to do with him — because the evidence is overwhelming that it was the CFR, operating as usual far behind the scenes, that "invented" Jimmy Carter for the 1976 election, as it "invented" Henry Kissinger to protect its interests under Richard Nixon.

Jimmy first came to the attention of the Shadow Government in 1970 — not by winning the governorship of Georgia, but by demonstrating *after* the election that he could be as devious and dishonest as any New York banker. By the time his face appeared on the cover of CFR-controlled *Time* in 1971, some very important people were watching him with interest.

In late 1972, a Harvard professor named Milton Katz received a telephone call from "the grand old man of the

Democrats," W. Averell Harriman. Harriman, whose service to internationalism dates back to 1922, when he helped arrange some crucial financing for the Bolshevik conquest of Russia, called Katz's attention to a rising young southerner, Jimmy Carter. CFR-member Harriman knew that fellow-CFR-member Katz had important connections: as a director of the Ford Foundation, the World Affairs Council, the World Peace Foundation, and chairman of the Carnegie Endowment for International Peace (four of the most important groups in the country promoting one-world government), Katz could certainly help a deserving young man get ahead.

Katz delivered like a slot machine hitting the jackpot; he arranged to introduce Carter to David Rockefeller. The talented Rockefeller, who is chairman of both the CFR and the ultra-influential Chase Manhattan Bank, has been called the most powerful man in the world.* It was an auspicious moment for the Georgia crackerjack.

In the fall of 1973, David invited Jimmy to have dinner with him in London. Over the *hors d'oeuvres*, David asked Jimmy to become a member of the Trilateral Commission — an important new group David was forming to promote world government. By the time dessert was served, Jimmy had agreed to come on board. The Trilateral Commission is another CFR front (over half of its 65 North American members also belong to the CFR); its purpose, according to Rockefeller, is "to bring the best brains in the world to bear on the problems of the future" — which is Rockespeak for the creation of a World Government.

---

* For the complete story of the Rockefellers' incredible power, influence, and ambition, see *The Rockefeller File* by this author. (1976: '76 Press, Seal Beach, Calif.)

The founding Director of David's Trilateral Commission was Dr. Zbigniew Brzezinski; he is, of course, a member of the CFR. If you find his name hard to pronounce, we suggest you practice it — for by 1976 Brzezinski had emerged as Carter's chief adviser on foreign affairs and the odds-on favorite to dictate U.S. foreign policy in a Carter Administration. Henry Kissinger has called Brzezinski my "distinguished presumptive successor," and admits that Carter's foreign policy pronouncements are almost carbon copies of his own. If you like Kissinger, you'll love Brzezinski!

Brzezinski, with Carter's blessing, assembled *quite* a team for the Boy Wonder from Plains. As reported in the June 24, 1976 issue of the *Los Angeles Times*, here are Carter's key task force members and foreign policy advisers: Zbigniew Brzezinski of Columbia University; the United Nations' major American propagandist, Richard N. Gardner; Richard Cooper of Yale University; Henry Owen of the Brookings Institution, an Establishment "think tank;" Edwin O. Reischauer, former U.S. Ambassador to Japan; retired diplomat W. Averell Harriman; Anthony Lake, a former aide to Henry Kissinger; Harvard professors Robert Bowie, Milton Katz, and Abram Chayes; former Undersecretary of State George Ball; and, former Secretary of the Army Cyrus R. Vance. It would be worth noting if Carter tapped even three or four CFR insiders to help him. But *every person on the list* is a member of the Council on Foreign Relations!

As *Newsweek* magazine reported on June 21 of this year, Jimmy Carter is far from being an opponent of the Liberal Establishment:

> *Despite the anti-Washington tone of his campaign, a surprising number of Carter advisers are old Washington hands. Joseph Califano, a top LBJ*

aide, and Theodore Sorensen, JFK's close adviser, will recommend appointments to a Carter Administration. Johnson's former Secretary of Defense, Clark Clifford, will advise the reorganization task force. Other counselors come from Washington's Brookings Institution (frequently referred to as the Democratic government-in-waiting) and that epitome of Eastern establishmentarianism, New York's Council on Foreign Relations.

By this time, we hope you will *not* be surprised to learn that Califano and Sorensen are CFR members. And while Clifford is not, his Establishment credentials are otherwise impeccable.

But the above list is by no means complete. Added to it should be the names of such major Carter advisers and supporters as: Bayless Manning, president of the CFR; SALT negotiator Paul Nitze; LBJ adviser Paul Warnke; Richard Holbrooke, editor of *Foreign Policy* magazine; former Air Force Secretary Thomas K. Finletter; Michael Forrestal, a lawyer for big New York investment firms; Alexander C. Trowbridge, Jr., a former Esso (now Exxon) executive who, as Commerce Secretary, helped open the floodgates for shipping strategic goods to the Communist bloc *on credits guaranteed by Washington*; Gerard Smith, onetime chairman of the Arms Control and Disarmament Agency; and Yale law professor Eugene Rostow. Every single one is a member of the CFR.

Other CFR members who have helped make Jimmy what he is today include those early contributors to his campaign, Dean Rusk, C. Douglas Dillon, Henry Luce, and Cyrus Eaton. Hail, hail, the gang's all here!

Syndicated columnist Paul Scott, one of the few

reporters with the courage to blow the whistle on the Rockefeller-CFR combine, confirmed Carter's close working relationship with the insiders' Godfather, David Rockefeller, in this July 7 report:

> *Most intriguing political connection of former Georgia Governor Jimmy Carter is his relationship with international banker David Rockefeller, one of the most influential men in the world.*
>
> *. . . Carter was picked several years ago to serve on the Trilateral Commission, which was organized by Rockefeller to study problems of common interest to the U.S., Western Europe, and Japan.*
>
> *The first director of the Commission was Zbigniew Brzezinski, a long-time associate of the Rockefeller family and now Carter's number one foreign policy adviser.*
>
> *. . . Friends of Brzezinski describe him as close to David Rockefeller as is the present Secretary of State Henry Kissinger to David's brother, Vice President Nelson Rockefeller.*

David Horowitz, author of *The Rockefeller Dynasty* and a reporter with solid-brass Liberal credentials, has said that the interconnection of Rockefeller, Brzezinski, and Carter is "very close." Yes, the Carter bandwagon runs on Standard Oil, not peanut oil. He and Rockefeller are as close as two peanuts in a shell.

With friends like these, it is possible to arrange all sorts of amazing "coincidences." Does the CFR want their man to get more attention in the media than any other candidate? Simply turn on the spigot, and paens of praise to Smilin' Jim roll off the presses.

Want to show how it is possible to butter both sides of a peanut at the same time? Viola! You have Leonard Woodcock, dictatorial chief of the United Auto

Workers, and Henry Ford II, the *creme de la creme* of big business, both endorse Carter *on the very same day*. (But please don't reveal that Woodcock and Ford are both members of the CFR, or that Woodcock also shares a seat with Carter on the Trilateral Commission. You don't want to give away the game, do you?)

Need a Vice President to go with him? How about a leftist Senator from Minnesota who is a member of both the CFR and the Trilateral Commission? When the envelope is opened, out pops Walter Mondale.

Jimmy Carter has been picked by the powers-that-be as *their* man to ride the wave of the future. To make sure he keeps his surfboard headed in the right direction, they have already surrounded him with veteran campaigners in their march to a New World Order. And Jimmy is proving he is a *very* willing recruit.

It is no coincidence, therefore, that Carter's two major foreign policy addresses during the primary campaign were both delivered to CFR front groups — the first, before the Chicago Council on Foreign Relations in March; the second before the Foreign Policy Association in New York in June. In both speeches, Carter repeatedly used such CFR code phrases as "a just and peaceful world order" and "a new international order." Those good ol' boys back in Georgia might not have known what was going on, but you can be certain that the makers and shakers in New York, Washington, and a dozen foreign capitals realized precisely what signals were being flashed to them.

James Reston of the *New York Times*, who is probably the top media insider, said it was "reassuring" to hear young Jimmy echoing "the basic theme of Woodrow Wilson and the League of Nations, of Roosevelt and Truman at the founding of the United Nations in San Francisco . . . ." It was the same old shell game; only this time it was being played with peanuts, not walnuts.

Conservative columnist Jeffrey Hart saw the shells being switched, but even he didn't realize how thoroughly we marks are being suckered:

> *In the primaries, [Carter] ran as a critic of the establishment and of the Washington bureaucracy. He was a totally unfamiliar figure, and he seemed to represent the South, including the Sun Belt. As he rolled on toward the nomination, he gave the inhabitants of the Cambridge-New York-Washington axis some sleepless nights. They know now that he is going to save their bacon.*

Carter's speech at the United Nations on May 13, declaring that "Balance of power politics must be supplemented by world order politics;" his comments before the Chicago Council on Foreign Affairs condemning "the strident and bellicose voices of those who would have this country return to the day of the cold war with the Soviet Union;" his pledge to the Foreign Policy Association in New York to work for "a just and peaceful world order;" Dr. Brzezinski's declaration to Democratic Congressmen that "We have to establish some sort of global equity" — such messages were more welcome to the audiences they were addressing than an interest-free loan from Chase Manhattan Bank. Needless to say, this is hardly the rhetoric of a Georgia goober-grower who just happened to be visiting a big Yankee city.

The few foreign-policy specifics that Carter has expressed could have been written in the New York offices of the CFR. (In fact, they probably were!) He has said, for example, that he would remove our troops from Europe and Korea, strengthen the United Nations, promote international controls of all atomic power, yield "part" of our sovereignty over the Panama Canal, kill the B-1 bomber, slash $5 to $7 billion from our defense budget, and increase foreign aid.

The accent may come from Georgia, but the words are straight from the CFR.

Only a select handful of insiders are supposed to get the message, of course. The fodder that has been prepared to keep the rest of us sheep happily munching, while we're herded into a Rockefeller-CFR world government corral, comes cleverly disguised.

The following editorial from the Scripps-Howard newspaper, the *Fullerton Daily Tribune*, is typical:

> *Rarely has a politician rocketed from obscurity to capture a presidential nomination as has Jimmy Carter, lately an out-of-office peanut farmer in Plains, Ga., and now the morning line favorite to win the White House.*
>
> *His feat is all the more remarkable in that he did it with only a small band of disciples in Atlanta and without early help from Democractic party power brokers — congressional leaders, governors, big city mayors, labor chiefs, and wealthy contributors.*
>
> *As a result Carter is unusually free of obligations, owing as he does his nomination mostly to himself. "Nobody has hooks in Carter," as the politicos put it elegantly and thus if elected, his policies would be set by his own desires and conscience.*

Sure. There is about as much chance of James Earl Carter, Jr. double-crossing the Establishment that has made him, as there is of Richard Nixon winning a clean government award. And if, for some reason, the peanut politico *does* decide to switch sides once again, he will learn — as have other politicians before him — how quickly the Shadow Government can turn a proud peacock into a discarded feather duster.

7 On To The Presidency

Most of the delegates to this year's Democratic Convention got a chance to sleep late Thursday morning. Nothing would be happening at Madison Square Garden until late afternoon. The faithful would turn on their televisions at ten o'clock, of course, to learn who The Man had picked as his running mate. But there really wasn't much else to get up for.

Even the late-night partying seemed strangely constrained this year. One exception was the madcap affair sponsored by *Rolling Stone* magazine, the counterculture tabloid that is usually in orbit somewhere around Mars. (It's endorsement of Carter three months earlier, "with fear and loathing," read like the ravings of a man attempting self-embalmment with bourbon — probably because it was.) *Rolling Stone*'s very liquid celebration, which had people lined up three blocks deep waiting to get in, was "the glittering social event of the convention."

Six persons who *were* up bright and early that muggy Thursday morning were the nominees-in-waiting. So were the cameramen and technicians, who readied the equipment that would carry Carter's announcement around the world. When the real Vice Presidential candidate was asked to stand up, the one who moved was Walter "Fritz" Mondale.

Many observers were surprised at the choice: Jimmy

had reached so far to the left in Washington, he was halfway to West Virginia. But, as we have noted before, the ultra-liberal Mondale was the *first* choice of the Establishment. A member of both the Council on Foreign Relations and Rockefeller's Trilateral Commission, Mondale had never been known to vote against Big Government — or in favor of free enterprise. His voting record, as tabulated by the far-left Americans for Democratic Action, was actually five points to the *left* of George McGovern. As titular head of the Farm Labor Party in Minnesota (which is far to the left of the national Democratic Party), Mondale would help unite the big unions behind the ticket. And he could generate a real excitement among liberal activists who thus far mostly had sat on their placards.

So there was Jimmy Carter, the man with the gleaming white teeth and the former red neck, declaring that, "I feel completely compatible with Senator Mondale." He would be the best person to succeed me as President, the ostensible conservative said. And besides, "there are no discernible differences" between his positions and mine. (Yes, Cornelia, this is the same man who said four years ago, "I think you will find . . . George Wallace and I are in agreement on most issues.")

The "Grits and Fritz in '76" ticket was off and running. UAW President Leonard Woodcock promised "the greatest united labor effort that this country has ever seen." Months earlier, AFL-CIO Secretary-Treasurer Lane Kirkland had promised that, if Carter won the nomination, "we'll find virtues in him his own mother didn't know he had."

So would almost everyone else. At the Democratic Convention, Carter achieved incredible harmony by making whatever promises were necessary to every conceivable pressure group: Blacks, Chicanos, labor, farmers, women's libbers and gays all jumped aboard the goober wagon in the belief that, once elected, Carter would pay off like a slot machine that just rang up five lemons. But no matter what the toilers in Carter's peanut patch believe, the party of Jefferson and Jackson will be controlled from behind the scenes by Chase Manhattan and Exxon. To paraphrase John Kennedy, "Ask not what Jimmy Carter can do for you, ask what he *will* do for David Rockefeller."

Walter Mondale's dowry for the nationally televised wedding was quite impressive: As the original sponsor of legislation providing public funds for Presidential elections, he had set the wheels in motion that meant the Carter-Mondale ticket would have $21.8 million from the taxpayers to spend between now and November on getting elected.

Carter had already demonstrated that he was eager to start. Back in June, he revealed that he may have *several* proposals to put before Congress *even before he assumes office*. A delegation from Plains, Georgia made plans to visit Johnson City, Texas to see how another small southern city adjusts to having a hometown boy in the White House. And Rosalynn Carter was already telling reporters how she planned to redecorate the Executive Mansion, come next January.

Will Jimmy Carter become the thirty-ninth President of the United States? We are not tuned in to any psychic wavelengths; we leave predictions to the seers and clairvoyants like Jeanne Dixon.

But the truth is unmistakable that, as of this moment, the Pepsodent Peanut is the odds-on favorite to defeat *any* ticket the Republicans nominate in Kansas City. We believe such an outcome could be a tragedy.

We admit that we have long been suspicious of public officials who amass huge power (not to mention considerable fortunes) while proclaiming, "Trust me." We agree instead with the solemn warning by one of the Democrats' founding fathers, Thomas Jefferson, who said: "In questions of power, then, let no more be heard of confidence in man, but bind him down from mischief by the chains of the Constitution."

The author of the Declaration of Independence was also familiar with another Carter trait: "He who permits himself to tell a lie once, finds it much easier to do it a second and third time, till at length it becomes habitual; he tells lies without attending to it, and truths without the world's believing him."

The problem with Jimmy Carter is not that he twists the truth like a farm wife wringing a chicken's neck, but that he does it while piously swearing to be completely honest. Thanks to a press that is so sympathetic it is almost fawning, he *seems* completely believable — even when his remarks bear as little relation to the truth as a Picasso painting does to its subject.

Back in June 1972, when the ambitious young governor was trying to halt McGovern's march to the nomination, Jimmy wrote an article warning:

> It's almost inconceivable to me that Democratic convention delegates could nominate a candidate who . . . favors amnesty for draft evaders, $1,000 government handouts to every American and a social spending program which would mount up federal deficits of more than $100 billion while undermining our defense capability . . . .

But that is *exactly* what happened in New York City this July! As we have seen, Jimmy Carter's domestic program is so liberal he makes George McGovern look like Calvin Coolidge. While his foreign policy pronouncements have been lifted, almost word for word, from the Rockefeller-CFR planning papers for World Government. His goal, as the *Christian Science Monitor* reported on June 24, is to build "a new international order."*

Here at home, it looks like the Graftathon has already begun. While Jimmy was beguiling his audiences with promises to bring back morality and integrity to government, his assistant, former McGovern staffer Patrick Caddell, was already ladelling from the gravy train.

Cambridge Reports, Inc., which is 35-percent owned by Caddell, is the beneficiary of *quite* a contract with the Royal Saudi Arabian Embassy. For $50,000 a year, cash in advance, the Saudis receive quarterly reports on American public opinion (a service they could obtain by subscribing to the daily papers). It is two-and-one-half times the rate paid by others for what Caddell calls a "subscription" to his services. For an extra $30,000 (total, $80,000 a year), the Saudis also bought the right to have thirty questions of their choice added to their "report."

In addition, columnist William Safire reported on July 21, Caddell's firm receives $80,000 a year from Exxon, Arco, Shell, and Sun for the "report."

Caddell has had to register as an official agent for a foreign power. But, Carter's staffer insists his $160,000 in oil money will in no way influence anybody or anything. And the self-righteous candidate sees no potential conflict of interest in having his assistant on the payroll of the world's oil biggies. Ah, yes, the Establishment takes care of its own — even when they must appear to be *so* anti-Establishment.

---

* At the convention, I asked Carter's press secretary, Jody Powell, what the Prince of Peanuts means by his constantly repeated phrase, "a new international order." Powell ducked the question by saying, "I don't think anyone knows what that means." You can bet your last quart of Exxon that David Rockefeller does!

Is this what the Democrats thought they were getting, when they nominated Carter by acclamation at their convention? Of course not. The simple truth is that Mr. Clean has not come clean about what he really intends to do. Kingsbury Smith, national editor of the Hearst newspaper chain, revealed that many persons who have not succumbed to the Carter charisma are convinced he is "a hypocritical opportunist who sacrifices principles for expediency and who has hoodwinked people by his personal charm and professions of honesty, love and godliness."

That may be what it takes for an ambitious politician to climb almost overnight from the Georgia Senate to the governor's mansion to the nomination for President of the United States. Such ruthless determination may even carry him into the White House. Reg Murphy, former *Atlanta Constitution* editor, is convinced it will. "He will win this presidential campaign because he's more determined to win than anybody else," Murphy says. "He will do what it takes to win; he will change what views it takes for him to win." And to make sure no one misses his point, Murphy adds, "He's absolutely ruthless."

But a ruthless, truthless candidate is the exact opposite of what Jimmy Carter has led voters to expect. They believe he will live up to the words of his own autobiography, "There is a simple and effective way for public officials to regain public trust — be trustworthy."

We think there is an even better way for the American people to get the kind of government they want: by *not* trusting politicians. In this Bicentennial year, if there is one hard-learned lesson from our Founding Fathers that should be printed in every textbook and inscribed on every ballot box, it is: "Don't trust government . . . or the men who run it."

We are well aware, as we write these concluding pages, that this book will be denounced by the keepers of the national press as political pornography; it will be condemned as a vicious and unwarranted smear and a despicable piece of contemptible journalism. They will not point out where our facts are wrong; they will count on their use of emotionally loaded catchwords to distract readers from accepting the truth.

We will probably even be accused of fronting for the Republicans — of trying to insure that the GOP wins the election this November by whatever means, fair or foul.

The truth is that this is a book we would have preferred not to write. We wish it were possible to believe that Jimmy Carter will build a New Jerusalem on the shores of the Potomac. We wish we could have the faith in him he asks us to have. But we have looked too carefully at the record to buy even a used peanut grinder from him. And we remember the admonition of Swiss philosopher Henri-Frederic Amiel: "Truth is violated by falsehood, but it is outraged by silence."

Nor are we fronting for the Republicans. Our earlier books on the Rockefeller control of the Grand Old Party make that clear.* We have no political axe to grind, no political candidate we are endorsing.

It is possible that Jimmy Carter's actions, if he is elected President, will be no better and no worse than his record as governor. Which would put him on a par with most of his predecessors in the Oval Office this century.

But we do know there is a way to make certain that our next President, whoever it may be, does not break his promises or betray his public trust. It requires an elec-

---

* See *None Dare Call It Conspiracy* (written in 1972), *The Rockefeller File* (written in 1975), and *Kissinger: The Secret Side of the Secretary of State* (written in 1976).

torate that *cares* about the issues — about the fate of their country, about the kind of future their children will inherit.

The solution is simply to apply the age-old truth, "eternal vigilance is the price of liberty," to the present political process. It means watching what politicians *do*, not just listening to what they say. It means keeping informed about important legislation; it means being knowledgeable about federal policies and programs. It means electing Congressmen who share your views — and then *watching* them (and keeping in touch with them) after they reach Washington.

One letter from you to one public official, written *after* the elections, can have more influence than ten votes this November. You *can* make certain that the next President and the new Congress not only talk but act to preserve the liberties we have inherited. You have everything it takes: paper, a pen, and some postage stamps. With these simple tools you and your neighbors can decide this country's future. We hope you will use them.

Freedom is not just being stolen by wealthy one-world monopolists and greedy special-interest groups. It is eroding by default, because so few people care enough to learn what is really going on. Americans are losing their capacity for indignation at governmental wrongdoing. We expect a truth-in-packaging law to apply to our cereal, but we set no such standards for our politicians. And yet, as the English philosopher Edmund Burke observed: "All that is necessary for the triumph of evil is for good men to do nothing."

What will you do?

After reading this book, you will never look at national and world events in the same way again.

Over four million copies of this explosive best seller have been distributed since it first appeared four years ago. It became one of the most widely read books in the country— without the benefit of a single review, advertisement, or promotion in the mass media.

The reason for its phenomenal success is that for the first time, someone had stated—and assembled the facts to prove —that conspiratorial forces behind the scenes actually control our government and dictate its policies. Read it and judge it for yourself!

1 copy — $1.00	25 copies — $10.00
3 copies — $2.00	100 copies — $30.00
10 copies — $5.00	1,000 copies — $250.00

Use order blank on the last page

The politician with one hand on the Bible and the other behind his back — with his fingers crossed!

JIMMY CARTER
JIMMY CARTER

by Gary Allen

An unauthorized biography of the slickest politician in America.

A veteran reporter blows the shell off the peanut politician from Plains, Georgia.

JIMMY CARTER/JIMMY CARTER contains all the unsavory facts that were carefully supressed during the Carter media blitz — the tall tales, exaggerated claims, broken promises, and dirty tricks that made Jimmy Carter an overnight sensation.

Here is the book that shows how Presidential candidates are created by the secretive Council on Foreign Relations and the national media which it controls.

Here is the exposé that is sure to be the controversial best seller of the year!

Plan to order extra copies of these three classic studies of the uses and abuses of great power and wealth.

'76 PRESS
P.O. Box 2686
Seal Beach, Calif. 90740

Please rush me the number of copies of **None Dare Call It Conspiracy** I have circled below:

1 copy - $1.00	25 copies - $10.00
3 copies - $2.00	100 copies - $30.00
10 copies - $5.00	1,000 copies - $250.00

Please rush me the number of copies of **The Rockefeller File** I have circled below:

1 copy - $1.95	50 copies - $50.00
5 copies - $8.75	100 copies - $75.00
10 copies - $15.00	500 copies - $325.00
25 copies - $31.25	1,000 copies - $500.00

Please rush me the number of copies of **Kissinger: The Secret Side of the Secretary of State** I have circled below:

1 copy - $1.50	100 copies - $60.00
10 copies - $12.50	500 copies - $250.00
50 copies - $45.00	1,000 copies - $400.00

Please complete the shipping information on the other side of this form and include payment with your order.

('**76 Press** will pay postage and handling charges when payment accompanies the order.)

Order Copies For Your Friends!

'76 Press
P.O. Box 2686
Seal Beach, Calif. 90740

Please rush me the number of copies of **Jimmy Carter/Jimmy Carter** I have circled below:

1 copy - $1.00
10 copies - $7.50
50 copies - $30.00
100 copies - $50.00
500 copies - $200.00
1,000 copies - $350.00

Amount of order

Jimmy Carter/Jimmy Carter	$_____
None Dare Call It Conspiracy	$_____
The Rockefeller File	$_____
Kissinger: The Secret Side of the Secretary of State	$_____
California residents: add 6% sales tax	$_____
TOTAL AMOUNT ENCLOSED	$_____

(**'76 Press** will pay postage and handling charges when payment accompanies the order.)

Name _____

Address _____

City _____ State _____ Zip _____